The Harrowsmith
Fish & Seafood
COOKBOOK

By the Editors & Readers of Harrowsmith Magazine

Compiled from the private recipe collections of the Editors,
Readers, Contributors and Staff of *Harrowsmith*,
Canada's National Award-Winning Magazine of
Country Living and Alternatives

FIREFLY BOOKS

A FIREFLY BOOK

Copyright © 1998 Firefly Books Ltd.

First published in 1985 by Camden House Publishing (a division of Telemedia Communications Inc.)

Seventh printing 2002

U.S. Publisher Cataloging-in-Publication Data
 (Library of Congress Standards) is available.

National Library of Canada Cataloguing in Publication Data
Main entry under title:

The Harrowsmith fish & seafood cookbook

Includes index.
ISBN 0-920656-38-2

1. Cookery (Fish).   2. Cookery (Seafood).
I. Cross, Pamela.   II. Pitt, Alice.
III. Collins, Winston, 1937 -   IV. Harrowsmith

TX747.H37   1985   641.6'9   C85-099489-6

Cover illustration by Roger Hill

Published by
Firefly Books Ltd.
3680 Victoria Park Avenue
Toronto, Ontario
Canada M2H 3K1

Published in the U.S. by
Firefly Books (U.S.) Inc.
P.O. Box 1338, Ellicott Station
Buffalo, New York 14205

Printed and bound in Canada by
Friesens
Altona, Manitoba

Printed on acid-free paper

The Harrowsmith Fish & Seafood
COOKBOOK

Editors
PAMELA CROSS, ALICE PITT

Text by
WINSTON COLLINS

Photography
ERNIE SPARKS

Design & Layout
PHILIP WOOD

Food Design
PAMELA WIMBUSH, ALICE PITT

Illustrations
COURTESY MINISTRY OF FISHERIES & OCEANS

Copy Editors
DAWNE SMITH, CHARLOTTE DuCHENE,
CATHERINE DeLURY, JOHN ARCHIBALD

Typesetting
PATRICIA DENARD

Photography Credits
PHOTOGRAPHIC PROPERTIES COURTESY OF:
KITCHEN CARGO, 86 BROCK ST., KINGSTON, ONTARIO
KEIRSTEAD GALLERY LTD., 166 PRINCESS ST., KINGSTON, ONTARIO
WILTON POTTERY, WILTON, ONTARIO
McMAHON'S HOUSE OF FLOWERS, 117 PRINCESS ST., KINGSTON, ONTARIO
ROBERT REID & SONS LTD., 230 PRINCESS ST., KINGSTON, ONTARIO

Contents

Introduction

What is the great globe itself but a Loose-Fish? And what are you, reader, but a Loose-fish and a Fast-Fish, too?

— Moby-Dick
Herman Melville

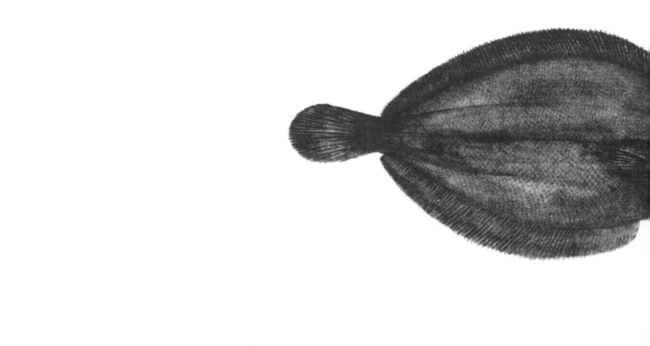

Raised on a landlocked dairy farm thousands of miles from the sea, I was born and bred a meat and potatoes eater. During my youth, eating fish was a rare, even alien, event. True, a can of salmon was usually on the pantry shelf; however, a more appropriate place would have been in the medicine cabinet. Mixed into a flour-paste sauce and served on white-bread toast, the processed fish was, as my mother put it, "sick food" — something to eat when the digestive system was in a state of rebellion.

But our family always had fish for Christmas dinner. In honour of my mother's Scandinavian heritage, *lutefisk* — ancient dried cod soaked in a lye solution — was the annual festive main dish. To the thoroughly North Americanized youngsters at the table, the slimy foreign substance, which had the power to turn silver forks black on contact, smelled and tasted worse than medicine. We gorged ourselves on Swedish meatballs instead. Other than an occasional Friday night all-you-can-eat fish fry at the local greasy spoon, that pretty well sums up the remembrance of my distant seafood past.

Sociologists say that our eating habits are governed by tradition. For most of us, eating fish is an exception, not a custom. Although Canada has more than a million lakes, innumerable streams and rivers, a coastline that stretches 150,000 miles along three oceans, and exports more fish than any other country in the world, we are a nation of carnivores. Canadians consume annually, per person, 92 pounds of beef and veal, 62 pounds of pork, 50 pounds of poultry, and a measly 13 pounds of fish. Though I've never calculated the weight of the food I eat, I'd estimate my current yearly consumption to be the exact reverse of the national meat-fish norm. For in spite of my beef-laden past, I am now a staunch fish lover.

DISCOVERING FISH

My conversion to fish took place at a steakhouse in Mexico. In the excitement of my first trip to a foreign country — and under the influence of two Tequila Sunsets — I ordered red snapper, the restaurant's fish-of-the-day, instead of rib-eye steak, the house specialty. It was, for a lad just off the farm, a daring choice. But the fresh fish, simply grilled and served on a silver platter, was a revelation. I had never imagined that fish could command such respect — or taste so good. Instantly, I was transformed into an icthyophagist, which I found out many years later is the erudite term for a devoted eater of fish.

My sea change in Mexico launched an ongoing quest for new piscatorial pleasures. Exotic encounters with the finny tribe are not hard to come by: after all, at least 21,000 species of fish inhabit the world's lakes, rivers and seven seas. Over the years, I've savoured grilled sardines in Greece, wind-dried salmon in British Columbia, raw sea urchins in Barbados, poached eels in Belgium, charred catfish in Louisiana. While the Mexican red snapper served on a silver platter still remains the most influential fish in my life, the best fish I have ever eaten was a cod fillet pan-fried in a cast-iron skillet in a Newfoundland kitchen.

The cod was cooked by a fisherman who had caught the cold-blooded grey-green creature in the Atlantic Ocean less than an hour earlier. As soon as he had plucked the cod from the water he knew it was a choice catch: "Now that's a beautiful fish, boy — fat and chunky, not thin and long." Gutting the fish on the outport wharf confirmed the cod's excellence: the fisherman declared that the liver was large and just the right shade of brown. For me, though, the codfish's true beauty was most clearly perceived when I tasted the white, odourless, delicately sweet and succulent fillet, which had been cooked simply and briefly on the kitchen stove.

My fisherman-host in the Newfoundland outport practises what is Canada's oldest profession. Cod fishing, the country's first industry, dates back to 1497, when John Cabot, the Venetian-born explorer and navigator, sailed the *Mathew* from Bristol, England, to the uncharted coast of Newfoundland. As an employee of Henry VII, Cabot was in search of a western passage to India; but instead of finding a new route to Asia's gems and spices, he discovered the North American continent and, with it, a treasure trove of fish. When Cabot reported to his monarch that he had come upon new waters "swarming with fish," not a passage to India, the King was not at all displeased. Discovering a cornucopia of cod then was like discovering a massive reservoir of offshore oil today.

Soon the waters off the newfound land, which England claimed as its own, were crowded with Portuguese, Spanish and French as well as English fishing vessels. In the late 1600s, fishermen were harvesting 100,000 metric tons of cod a year from Newfoundland's rich sea pastures; a century later, the annual catch reached 200,000 metric tons. International wars were waged for control of what was for 300 years the world's most important commodity; today, international wrangles continue over fishing rights in the North Atlantic's vast fishing banks — especially the fish-rich Grand Banks, which covers 175,000 square miles, most of which lies in the 200-mile offshore fishing zone set by Canada in 1977 as its exclusive management property.

We owe much of our heritage to the cod, which caused the British Navy to develop into the supreme masters of the waves and also spurred the growth of the ship-building industry in North America. In 1784, Massachusetts proclaimed the fish "Sacred Cod," and hung a huge carving of the aquatic animal on the Hall of Representatives. In Canada, cod was dubbed "Newfoundland currency." Some of the earliest European settlements in North America were established by fishermen along Newfoundland's coastline, where current place names recall the island's international past (English Harbour, Portugal Cove, Frenchman's Cove, Port-au-Basques) and the role fish played in its development (Fishing Ship Harbour, Caplin Cove, Herring Neck, Dog Fish Point, Schooner Island, Salmon Cove).

Eons before these communities, the earliest *Homo sapiens* established their settlements along shores of lakes, rivers and oceans, where fish evolved as a species nearly 500 million years ago. In comparison, *Homo erectus* is a mere whippersnapper, having come into being only two million years ago. Incidentally, most scientists believe that fish — the first animals to have a backbone — are our distant forebears. Whatever, archaeological evidence shows that early humans were fish eaters: Stone Age fishhooks fashioned from shells and bones look very much like those sold in fishing-supply stores today. Cave dwellers probably consumed their catch raw — but raw fresh herring was undoubtedly an improvement over grubs and locusts.

Fish was sustenance for ancient civilizations around the world. The Chinese caught their aquatic fare with spun-silk nets, while the Egyptians trapped theirs in nets woven from flax. Ancient Romans, who were partial to seafood served in spicy sauces, are credited with elevating fish cookery to an art. Although the art went into decline with the fall of the Roman Empire, the rise of Christianity kept fish eating and the fishing industry very much alive in Europe. The Church of Rome decreed Fridays and the 40 days of Lent to be times for abstaining from meat in favour of "bloodless" fish. Queen Elizabeth I went out of her way to support the British fishing industry: she declared that two days of each week, as well as Lent, should be meatless. To provide fish for the faithful, especially during the lengthy Lenten fast when fresh fish was hard to come by for most Europeans, preservation techniques were developed. The most common method by far was salting fish; indeed, until the 20th century, all the cod brought to Europe from the North Atlantic was salt preserved.

Long before foreign fishermen began salting fish on these shores, native peoples were preserving their catches by more delectable smoking and wind-drying techniques. In short, fish has been a mainstay in the human diet from time immemorial. But why are we so fish-shy today? The Japanese annually consume 150 pounds (measured in live weight) of fish per person; Norwegians, 100 pounds; Portuguese, 85 pounds. Canadians eat just 40 pounds of fish per person and Americans average 5 pounds less.

Are we really, as a radio commentator recently claimed, a nation of fish haters? Certainly not for long, as all the trends indicate a massive societal turning toward leaner, healthier foods. One reason we eat substantially less fish than meat, as

formal and informal studies show, is that we don't know how to prepare it. A second and more major reason ties in with the fear of fish cookery: we aren't in the habit of buying fish. For good health alone, it is a habit well worth developing. But to my mind, the best reason to discover fish is the pure pleasure of its taste. And believe it or not, mastering the art of fish cookery is simple. A salmon steak is easier to broil than a sirloin, and sautéing a cod fillet is child's play compared even to searing a medium-rare hamburger.

FISH GOODNESS

Fish has long been credited with possessing health-promoting powers. Ancient doctors recommended salted tuna as an antidote to snake bites and boiled shark brains as a cure for toothaches. In the 17th century, the British Royal College of Physicians gave its stamp of approval to using pike, in one form or another, to treat eye infections and feverish fits. A Newfoundland folk medicine remedy for rheumatism used to be an application of dissolved jellyfish; when patients complained that the smell was worse than the pain, the remedy was changed to wearing a haddock fin in an amulet around the neck. Within living memory, it has been claimed — sometimes with justification — that eating fish clears the skin, makes hair shine, improves vision and increases brain power. And as almost everyone knows, oysters are, like chocolate and liquor, a sure-fire aphrodisiac.

Although my mother considered fish "sick food," a more accurate label would be food for health. Fish and seafood are made-to-order for our contemporary health-and-fitness age. Packed with high-quality protein, fish is low in calories, cholesterol, fat and (surprisingly) sodium. No wonder health professionals are urging people concerned about their weight, their heart and their general well-being to eat more fish and less meat. According to one nutritionist's reckoning, a T-bone steak contains 20 percent protein calories and 80 percent fat calories, while fillet of sole's caloric count is 90 percent protein and 10 percent fat. As well, fish fat is unsaturated, unlike saturated animal fat, which has been linked to heart disease. Numerous studies have shown that countries with fish-oriented diets have a substantially reduced incidence of heart attack and stroke.

Fish and seafood are good sources of vitamin A, which keeps the skin, hair and eyes in good condition; vitamins B_6 and B_{12}, which help red blood cells develop and the nervous system to function properly; and vitamin D, which aids in building and maintaining healthy bones and teeth. Eating fish and seafood also provides the body's system with essential minerals: iodine (for the thyroid); copper (for red blood cells, connective tissue and nerve fibres); magnesium (for metabolism and bodily tissues); selenium (for the heart and digestive tract); fluorene and phosphorus (for strong bones and teeth). Fish canned with its bones — such as salmon or sardines — is an excellent source of calcium; mainly because of the edible bones, canned fish is a better source of minerals than fresh fish — and a far better source than red meat.

Consider the dietary goodness of 3 ounces of humble canned sardines compared to 3 ounces of boned choice sirloin. Both contain equal amounts of protein and iron, but the sirloin has almost twice as many calories and three times more fat. When it comes to vitamin A, sardines trounce sirloin 190 International Units (IUs) to

50 IUs, and the little fishes absolutely wallop the chunk of meat in calcium content, 372 mg to 9 mg.

BUYING & STORING BASICS

For many people, buying fish is a more intimidating undertaking than cooking it. The fresher the better is a familiar fish-buying maxim — but how can you know for sure if the aquatic animal on display is really fresh?

"If a fish doesn't look and smell right, it's not fresh," a fish dealer once told me. "Trust your senses." Here is an easy three-step sense test for determining fish freshness:

1. Look at the eyes: they should appear disconcertingly alive — bright, clear and bulging. Look, too, for moist skin, shiny scales that adhere tightly to the body and reddish gills.

2. Touch the body: fresh fish flesh will give slightly and then spring back into shape after it has been gently poked or firmly pressed by the finger.

3. Smell the fish: it should not have a "fishy" odour. Although some poetic fish lovers have likened the smell of fresh fish to that of cucumbers, celery, thyme and even wild violets, most nostrils discern virtually no odour at all — perhaps just a pleasant whiff of fresh water.

Fish in the marketplace comes in various forms. Since the terminology can be a bit mystifying, especially for the novice buyer, here are definitions of the forms fish take in the market.

Whole: The fish is completely intact — just as it existed in the water. (Since fish is best preserved if it is eviscerated or gutted as soon as possible this is a rare market form.)

Dressed, or drawn: The fish has been eviscerated and often scaled; otherwise it looks like a whole fish. (Most people would call this a cleaned fish; however, fishfolk don't like the suggestion that aquatic animals are ever unclean, hence the circumlocution.)

Pan-dressed: The fish has its entrails, scales, gills, head and often its tail and fins removed. As the name implies, it is ready for cooking.

Steaks: The cross-sections cut from large pan-dressed fish with part of the backbone attached.

Fillets: The meaty side portions cut lengthwise from a fish. (**Butterfly fillets** are the two side portions united by belly skin.) A fillet — which is pronounced fill-it, by the way — may or may not be skinned; it is almost always boneless, which makes it an excellent cut for people who fear fish because of its bones.

The next question is: How much fish to buy? Here is a guideline for 1 serving of fish, by weight: whole — 1 pound; dressed — 1 pound; pan-dressed — ½ pound; steaks — ½ pound; fillets — ⅓ to ½ pound. The serving portions can be reduced in size if the fish is stuffed or prepared in a heavy sauce.

Most fish forms displayed in the marketplace are steaks and fillets. Obviously, you can't gaze into their eyes; but they, too, should be subjected to and pass the look-touch-smell test: buy only cuts that look moist and glossy, respond elastically to the touch and smell (if they smell at all) like mild brine, not old socks.

Besides trusting your senses, find a trustworthy fish dealer who knows his suppliers and keeps his market immaculately clean. "A fisherman is one rogue, a merchant many," is an old Newfoundland saying still heard in the island's outports. Nevertheless, a reliable fishmonger who cares about topnotch fish and seafood and gets his products on the market as soon as possible can be your best friend when it comes to buying the best fare the waterworld has to offer.

The quicker a fish makes its way from the water to the table the better. While a little ageing improves beef, time is no friend of fish, whose fatty acids quickly become rancid when exposed to air. Consequently, fresh fish should always be preserved on ice in the refrigerator. Thanks to improved refrigeration and transportation techniques, high-quality fish is now available from coast to coast at almost any time.

Still, frozen fish is not to be sneered at. Paradoxically, the rock-hard commercial product is sometimes fresher than so-called fresh fish. For instance, a package of frozen fillets marked with the initials IQF (individually quick-frozen) can be a more reliable product than "fresh" fish, which may have spent untold days inside an ocean trawler before being deposited on a wharf, then moved to a plant, and, at long last, trucked to the hinterlands.

Although frozen fish is often more convenient to buy than fresh fish (and often cheaper, too), it is trickier to know precisely what you are getting, especially if the packaging makes the contents invisible. In this case, make sure the package is airtight; then squeeze it firmly — it should feel solidly frozen with no evidence of ice crystals within. When opened, the fish should look moistly shiny and have no discoloration or freezer-burn.

Bringing fish home: Fresh fish is best eaten the same day it is bought. (In an ideal world, it would be eaten the same day it is caught.) Julia Child, who has been dishing up sage food advice for the past 25 years, says fish should be the last item on the shopping list. Child recommends either buying fish just before coming home or taking a thermal container with ice to pack it in. As soon as fish enters your home, wipe it with a damp cloth, then wrap it tightly in plastic or foil and store it in the refrigerator, preferably surrounded by ice. But don't keep it there for long: a fresh fish becomes a long-in-the-tooth fish in just a couple of days.

If you don't intend to eat the fish within three days, you could freeze it at a temperature of at least -4 degrees F. As a rule, though, freezing market-bought fish at home is not recommended; commercial fish companies have the facilities to do the job more effectively and quickly. Freezing fish does not imbue the creature with immortality — most fish should be eaten within two months of freezing.

Whether frozen fish should be thawed before cooking is a point of debate among cooks. The cook-it-frozen school contends that thawed fish becomes mushy; the thaw-it-first advocates, of whom I'm one, argue that a frozen slab will not cook through properly. I have found that thawing fish overnight in the refrigerator — or, in a pinch, in a basin of cold water for an hour or so — enables fish to retain its texture and much of its quality. Though frozen fish is never as delectable as fresh-from-the-water fish, it is, as one icthyophagist remarked, a whole lot better than no fish at all.

Shellfish is one of the world's finest — and most perishable — delicacies. Most fresh shellfish must be alive and kept alive until it is eaten — an event that should take place within 12 hours of its purchase. As with fresh fish, use and trust your senses when buying any of the toothsome aquatic invertebrates.

Lobsters and crabs should look lively; buy those that move their legs vigorously when given a prod. Oysters, clams and mussels should not have broken shells; above all, the shells must be hard and tightly closed. Shrimp should be firm with shells that fit tightly to the bodies. Scallops are usually already out of their shells when they are on the market: choose those that look white and moist and have a pleasant, slightly sweet smell.

Store shellfish in the refrigerator in a dish lightly covered with a damp cloth — never in water or wrapped in plastic or foil. If bivalves should open while being stored, give them a firm rap; if they fail to close, discard them. Home-freezing is not recommended for shellfish. Commercially frozen shellfish is, at best, a far distant cousin to the real thing.

Because shellfish come in all sorts of sizes and are eaten in a diverse number of ways, guidelines for how much to buy are not carved in stone. But here are some rules of thumb for 1 serving: whole live lobster — 1½ pounds; crabmeat, out of the shell — ¼ pound; oysters on the half shell — 5 or 6; clams on the half shell — 6 to 8; mussels, in their shells — ¾ pound; shrimps — ½ pound; scallops — ¼ to ⅓ pound depending on the recipe.

Should you aspire to have your name in the *Guinness Book of Records*, these are the shellfish-gluttony feats you must surpass: clams — 424 in 8 minutes; shrimps — 3 pounds in 4 minutes, 8 seconds; oysters — 250 in 2 minutes, 52.33 seconds.

FISH COOKERY: QUICK & EASY

COOKING TIME

Fish lovers around the world are indebted to Canadian waters for such glorious fare as Arctic char, Digby scallops, Malpeque oysters, Maritime lobsters, Restigouche salmon and Winnipeg goldeye. But the nation's single greatest contribution to fish-eaters' well-being comes from an Ottawa kitchen — specifically, Canada's Department of Fisheries test kitchen, where the revolutionary "Canadian cooking theory" was formulated.

The theory's principle is simplicity itself: *Measure the depth of fish at its thickest point, and cook it for exactly 10 minutes per inch.* (For frozen fish, double the time to 20 minutes per inch.)

The trailblazing theory — which has become an established rule for many professional chefs and home cooks alike — applies to cooking any fish form (whole-dressed, pan-dressed, steaks and fillets) of any species of fish (but not shellfish) in any method whatsoever. James Beard, the late American chef, cooking teacher and food writer, proclaimed the Canadian cooking theory to be "probably the most important announcement in fish cookery of the last century"; the celebrated gourmet also declared that the technique "works like a charm and is completely foolproof."

In spite of Beard's unqualified endorsement, the Canadian cooking theory is meant to be a helpful guideline, not an absolute rule. Given the vagaries of individual stoves and the varying nature of fish flesh (absolutely fresh fish cooks exceptionally fast, for instance), it is a good practice to test fish *before* the allotted 10-minutes-per-inch cooking time has expired. Gently insert the tip of a sharp knife or the end of a metal skewer into the thickest part of the fish; when the fish is no longer translucent, it is ready to eat. Serve immediately.

To-the-minute timing is crucial to successful fish cookery. Unlike meat, fish cooks rapidly because it has very little connective tissue; exposed to prolonged heat, fish flesh breaks down, dries out and loses its flavour. So the first commandment of fish cookery is: *Do not overcook.* "Fish, like eggs, should be cooked quickly and lightly and served at once in its own odorous heat," advises M.F.K. Fisher, the doyenne of food writers.

The ease and quickness with which fish can be prepared make it the ultimate fast food. Unlike a Big Mac or Chicken Nugget, fish does not need doses of additional seasonings to give it flavour. Indeed, "the better the fish the simpler should be its preparation," is a wise dictum. Fish fresh from the water rarely calls for anything more than a twist of the pepper mill — and, if desired, a touch of salt and a squeeze of lemon — to complement its intrinsic good taste.

COOKING METHODS

Fish can be cooked quickly and easily in a variety of delectable ways: on or in the stove; over hot coals; immersed in oil, wine or water, or over a simmering liquid. Whatever the method, use the Canadian cooking theory as the timing guideline.

Baking

Baking is a particularly effective method of cooking whole dressed fish, thick steaks and large fillets. Preheat the oven to 450 degrees F. Place the fish on a greased baking dish to prevent sticking; to facilitate the handling and serving of a large fish, line the dish with greased foil. Sprinkle seasonings on top, if desired. When fish is baking in a sauce, add 5 minutes to the total cooking time. If cooked in a cream, egg or cheese sauce, bake slightly longer in a slower oven (350 degrees F).

One of the quickest, easiest and best dinners I know is freshly cut 1-inch halibut steaks — topped with ground pepper, minced garlic and sprigs of tarragon — baked for 10 minutes. Voila! – a superb main course that requires a total of just 12 minutes to assemble, cook and serve.

Poaching

Poaching is a fat-free method of cooking fish in simmering (not boiling) liquid. First, bring enough liquid to cover the fish to a boil. Add the fish; as soon as the liquid reaches the boiling point again, reduce heat so the liquid simmers steadily. Begin timing at the fish-added point; never let fish sit in the liquid when the cooking time expires.

Poaching liquids include classic Court Bouillon (white wine and water seasoned with aromatic herbs and chopped vegetables), a mixture of milk and water, which is a lovely hot bath for smoked fish, and just plain water. Small cuts of poached fish are easily managed in an ordinary pan; but a large fish or large pieces of fish are best coped with in a fish poacher, which comes equipped with a rack to hold and lift the fish so it doesn't break up. Alternatively, place large fish in a homemade cheesecloth "hammock," which is submerged into a deep roasting pan; keep the ends of the cloth free and dry to lift the cooked fish from the poaching liquid.

Steaming

Steaming is akin to poaching; however, steamed fish is cooked above, not in, simmering liquid. The most suitable cuts for fat-free steaming are fillets and steaks, as well as small whole fish. The popularity of Chinese cooking has made bamboo or stainless steel steamers familiar pieces of equipment in Canadian kitchens. Simply place the fish in the steamer rack; top with seasonings, if desired; and cook closely covered over simmering liquid for the allotted time.

Braising

Braising, like poaching and steaming, uses a cooking liquid — white or red wine, stock or a combination of both, depending on the recipe. First, cook finely cut vegetables (carrots, celery, onions) in butter until tender; put the vegetables in a baking dish or roaster and place the fish on top of the vegetables. Pour in the braising liquid to half cover the fish, cover the pan with a sheet of aluminum foil and cook slowly either on top of the stove or in an oven preheated to 350 degrees F. The braising vegetables and liquid can be made into an excellent sauce for the cooked fish, which may be left in the warm liquid for up to an hour before serving.

Foil-Wrapped Cooking

Cooking fish in an aluminum-foil package is often classified as a variation on baking, poaching, steaming or braising. In fact, though, it is a fusion of all four cooking methods. And because it is probably the most easily managed and one of the most flavourful ways of preparing fish, the technique deserves a special place of its own among cooking methods. Here's how it is done: Wrap a whole fish, or individual steaks or fillets, in packages made from well-greased heavy aluminum foil; seal tightly and bake on a cookie sheet at 450 degrees F for the appropriate time, adding on 5 minutes to enable the heat to penetrate the foil. (Before cooking, fish can be seasoned with herbs, diced vegetables and a splash of wine.) Foil-cooked fish is equally good hot, accompanied by a hollandaise sauce, or cold, served with homemade mayonnaise or a herb-laden tofu dressing.

Pan-frying

Pan-frying, or sautéing, is a particularly appealing technique for cooking lean fillets and steaks, as well as small whole fish. To seal in the juices, the fish is usually coated with flour or bread crumbs before it is quickly cooked in a moderately hot skillet greased with a mixture of butter and oil. The best fish I've ever tasted — fresh Newfoundland cod fillets cooked in a frying pan — was prepared in the classic pan-frying method: the fillets were first rinsed under cold running water and patted dry; they were then dipped in milk and then in flour seasoned with salt and pepper. The fillets were cooked in a skillet coated with 1 tablespoon of oil until golden brown on one side, turned and cooked until the opposite sides were golden brown as well. (If pan-fried fish seems a bit greasy, drain on paper towels before serving.)

Deep Frying

Deep frying lends itself to a wide variety of fish and shellfish. Fillets and small cuts of fish are the best choices. Coat the fish with a breading or batter and then submerge it in oil, preferably peanut or corn oil, which should be hot (375 degrees F) and deep enough (about 3 inches) to cover the fish. Drain well on paper towels before serving. *Oven frying* yields the same desirable crispness, but with fewer calories because less oil is used. Place the coated fish in a well-greased baking dish, top with a dribble of oil or melted butter and bake in a preheated oven of at least 450 degrees F.

Broiling

Broiling is a tasty method for cooking fillets and steaks, especially fresh cuts of such fat fish as salmon, lake trout and mackerel. Make sure the broiler unit is at full heat and the rack is well greased. Place the fish on the rack, baste with butter or oil and cook 3 to 4 inches below the unit. Fat fish usually doesn't need further basting, but lean fish benefits from a couple of moisturizing treatments during the intense cooking process. Thin fillets or steaks do not have to be turned, but pieces thicker than 1 inch should be turned at least once.

Barbecuing

Barbecuing fish over charcoal or wood coals produces a distinctive and delicious taste. Before the fish is placed on a clean and well-greased grill, the coals should be glowing hot. Baste the fish — thick steaks and whole or split fish are the best bets for this method — generously with oil, butter or special sauce before and during cooking on the grill, which should be 3 to 4 inches above the coals. To give fish an appealing woodland flavour, add chips of aromatic wood (e.g., mesquite, apple, alder or oak) to the hot coals about 5 minutes before you start cooking. By the way, barbecuing fish well is not a god-given talent for most of us — so never leave the fish unattended to go for a drink or check on the progress of the rest of the meal.

Raw Fish

Fish is such a versatile food that it need not be cooked at all to be delectable. Eating fish raw is a practice that is as old as the hills, and very much in vogue today. Fresh raw fish is the star ingredient of Japanese sushi, exquisite morsels of rice wrapped in seaweed which are currently a coast-to-coast rage. Scandinavian gravlax — raw salmon marinated for at least two days in a mixture of salt, sugar and lots of dill — has become a fashionable appetizer. An increasingly popular treat in North America is sevich, a Latin American dish of raw lean fish — or raw scallops and shrimps — cut into bite-sized pieces and marinated in lime or lemon juice; the citric acid actually "cooks" the fish in a matter of hours.

When it comes to cooking, fish is a remarkably adaptable creature indeed. Although some 200 different species are on the Canadian market, virtually all of them can be prepared in exactly the same ways. So if you come across a tempting recipe for poached sole fillets with a lemon and butter sauce but have no access to sole, simply substitute *any* fish fillets that are available and proceed with the recipe. While the kind of fish you use will determine a dish's taste, its ultimate success depends more on proper preparation than fish species.

Consider the cod, the most versatile of foods. On the Canadian market, the fish is sold fresh, frozen, cured and canned. In its frozen state, cod is marketed in the following forms: whole-dressed, pan-dressed, fillets, steaks, as well as in a block (either of pieces or minced) and as ready-to-cook fish sticks. Cod is also available smoked, dried, salted and in brine. Exotic byproducts include cod roe, cod cheeks and tongues.

In the kitchen, any kind of fish and seafood is notably adaptable, too. All edible species can be made into soups and chowders, pâtés and salads, fillings for sandwiches and omelettes, sauces for pasta and rice, hearty stews and casseroles, and elegant quenelles and mousses. Dressed up or straight-and-simple, fish is a catch you can always make the most of.

In cooking, fish and seafood have a natural affinity with spinach, tomatoes and asparagus, and with dill, tarragon, basil, garlic and lemons, as well. And of course, fish and wine — especially dry white wine — are the happiest of partners.

The French have a proverb, "*Poisson sans boisson est poison.*" (Fish without drink is poison.) For the French, "drink" means wine, just as, for Newfoundlanders, "fish" means cod.

FISH HEAVEN

I learned to love eating fish long before I learned to love cooking it. After my conversion to the gods of the sea, my temples of delight were restaurants that served superb fish dishes. Even now, my idea of fish heaven is a restaurant in Venice, the magical city that rides on water. It's called Trattoria Corte Sconta, an unpretentious place — as first-class fish restaurants almost always are — where butcher paper covers the long communal tables. Here the waiter might suggest you ignore the menu and, instead, allow him to deliver dishes of his choosing from the kitchen; when you've had enough, just tell him.

And what a parade of pleasures the Trattoria has in store. First, a procession of appetizers: warm scallops with their roe attached, a bowl of steamed baby clams, marinated sea snails, squid eggs, which is then followed by a platter of baby octopus garnished with baby shrimp and crabs. And then on to broiled grey mullet, grilled sardines, pasta with clams, grilled giant shrimp. Who knows when it will end? Who wants it to? But reluctantly you say, *Basta*! Enough!

CATCHING FISH TO EAT

When Mario Deviata, the owner and chef of Il Gabbiano, a fetching Italian seafood restaurant in Toronto, cooks a special dinner for guests at home, he serves smoked sturgeon garnished with marinated red peppers, followed by fettuccine with bay scallops. "And then I prepare a nice surprise — a grilled black bass I caught myself with a plastic worm," says the chef, who was born in Naples on the Mediterranean Sea, trained in hotels on Switzerland's lakes and a de-

cade ago began his Canadian restaurant career on the banks of the St. Lawrence River in Sept-Isles, Quebec. Deviata loves fishing so much that on occasion he'll hang a "Gone Fishing" sign on the locked door of his fish restaurant and head for a lake north of the city.

"Canada is one of the easiest countries in the world to catch fish," the angler-chef exclaims. Indeed, Canadian waters have yielded world-record-sized freshwater fish caught with a rod and reel: a 65-pound lake trout from Great Bear Lake, Northwest Territories; a 14-pound 8-ounce brook trout from the Nipigon River, Ontario; a 29-pound 11-ounce Arctic char from the Arctic River, Northwest Territories; a 31-pound coho salmon, from Cowichan Bay, British Columbia. World rod-and-reel saltwater records include a 46-pound lingcod, from Hakai Pass, British Columbia, and a 1,496-pound bluefin tuna, from Nova Scotia's coastal waters. The biggest fish on record is a 84,800-pound whale shark, from the Gulf of Siam; the oldest-known fish was a lake sturgeon from Wisconsin's Lake Winnebago, estimated to have lived to the age of 82.

Bigger and older does not mean better to anyone but the sport fisherman. Though record-sized fish might be impressive stuffed and hung in the rec room, they are no good stuffed and cooked in the kitchen. In any given species, smaller and younger fish are choicer food fare by far. They are also less likely to be affected by such dangerous contaminants as PCBs, mercury and pesticides than older and bigger freshwater fish. It is a sad but wise precaution today to know in advance which fish and waterbodies have been tested for pollutants, and what the results are. Before going fishing, check with your provincial department of the environment or natural resources.

The Ontario *Guide to Eating Sport Fish* offers practical advice on how to handle a catch: "Freshly caught fish should be chilled by placing on ice or under refrigeration as soon as possible. Then at the earliest opportunity, the fish should be cleaned, dressed and refrigerated or preserved for future use." Fisherman Mario Deviata, however, reverses the procedure: as soon as he catches a fish, he cleans or dresses it; then he immediately refrigerates his catch, which he keeps refrigerated until he seasons the dressed fish's cavity with chopped parsley, freshly ground pepper, salt and minced garlic, and places it on the grill. As a chef who specializes in "only the best from the sea," he knows that heat and air are a freshly caught fish's two worst natural enemies.

A FISH & SEAFOOD GUIDE

What's in a name? Very often confusion if it belongs to a fish. Marine nomenclature is, as the saying goes, a pretty kettle of fish — which is to say, a muddle. Flounder and sole are two well-known names on the Canadian fish market, but they are not necessarily two different fish. "Soles are always flounders, but flounders are not always soles," an official of Canada's Department of Fisheries and Oceans explains, sort of. Spiny dogfish, which is caught in abundance off the Atlantic coast, is often called harbor halibut in New England and rock salmon in Britain, where it is usually the fish in fish-'n'-chips; however, dogfish is neither a halibut nor a salmon, but a shark. Lingcod — a commercially important Pacific

Ocean fish sometimes known as blue cod, green cod, leopard cod and cultus cod — is, in fact, not a member of the cod family. Ever-popular ocean perch belongs to the rockfish, not the perch, family. And so it goes.

Even such everyday terms as fish and seafood can be confusing. To an Atlantic coast fisherman, the word "fish" means cod, nothing else, even though a dictionary defines a fish as any cold-blooded vertebrate that lives in water and breathes through its gills. Shellfish are quite another breed: they are either molluscs (soft-bodied invertebrates that generally have a hard shell, but sometimes have no shell whatsoever) or crustaceans (hard-shelled animals with jointed legs that usually, but not necessarily, live in water). Technically, seafood is the collective term for edible fish and shellfish. But in popular parlance, the term fish often includes shellfish as well; just as often, though, the term seafood refers to shellfish, as opposed to fish — which is the usage we've adopted for *The Fish and Seafood Cookbook*.

The following guide is designed to help clarify who's who in the fish market. Another aim is to provide a taste of the water world's immense variety of culinary delights. The guide is by no means a comprehensive compendium of fish and seafood; such an undertaking is well-nigh impossible because marine scientists keep discovering new aquatic creatures and adding them to the many thousands of species already identified.

Atlantic Salmon

    Salmon, according to food historians, is the world's oldest gourmet delight. Today, it ranks as Canadians' favourite fish. (Many people who profess not to like fish love salmon.) Most Canadian salmon is harvested near the shores of the Atlantic and Pacific oceans during the fat fish's spawning run to fresh-water streams and rivers, where it was born. **Atlantic salmon**, whose average weight is about 10 pounds, is mainly caught between May and August; the species is esteemed for its rich taste and firm texture.

Coho Salmon

Coho salmon is a popular sport and market fish. Due to its mostly silver colouring, it is also known as **silver salmon**. Its average weight is 4 to 10 pounds. To many icthyophagists, salmon is the perfect fish — it is certainly beyond compare in terms of cooking versatility.

Pink Salmon

Pink salmon is the smallest of the Pacific salmon, weighing from 3 to 5 pounds. It is easily recognized by large, oval spots on its back and its tail. It is generally canned but has a lighter pink colour than sockeye salmon.

Sockeye Salmon

Sockeye salmon is one of five kinds of salmon found in the Pacific waters off British Columbia. It is mainly canned as choice "red" salmon. Sockeyes weigh an average of 6 pounds and are caught throughout the summer months. Japan provides a large market for high-quality sockeye salmon from Canada.

English Sole

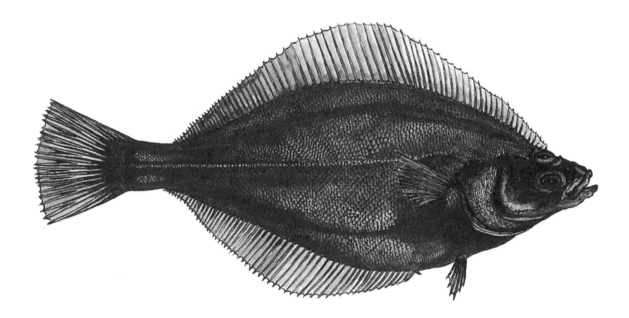

Flounder and **sole** are virtually interchangeable in marine terminology. "Flounder" is a catch-all term for a variety of flat fishes — fish with compressed bodies that swim on one side and have both eyes on their upper side. **English sole** is found in the shallow waters of the Pacific and is often called **lemon sole**, although it is not the same fish that is known by that name in Europe. The flesh is lean, white, firm and finely grained.

Rock Sole

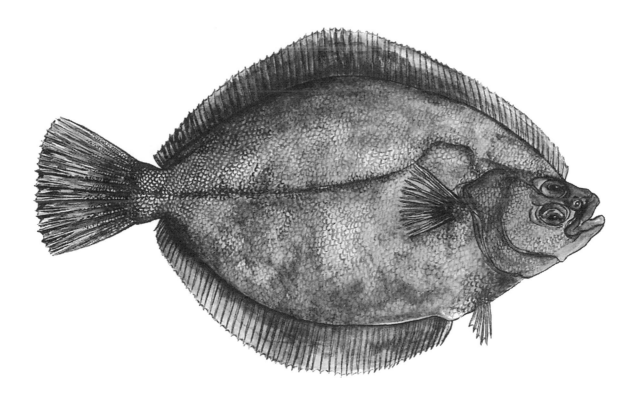

Rock sole is the most important of Canada's Pacific Ocean small flat fish. It has rough back scales, hence its other name — **roughback**. Very easily boned, rock sole may be cooked using any method — a common favourite is to pan-fry the sole fillets in butter and serve them with browned almonds.

Witch Flounder

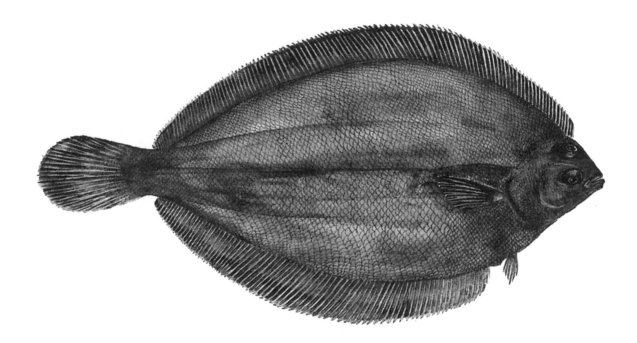

Witch flounder is yet another member of the sole/flounder family that is available in Canada. It is more commonly known as **greysole** because of its colouring. The average length of the witch flounder is 11 inches, with a weight of 1½ pounds. Sole/flounder comprise Canada's most important commercial groundfish catch next to cod.

Summer Flounder

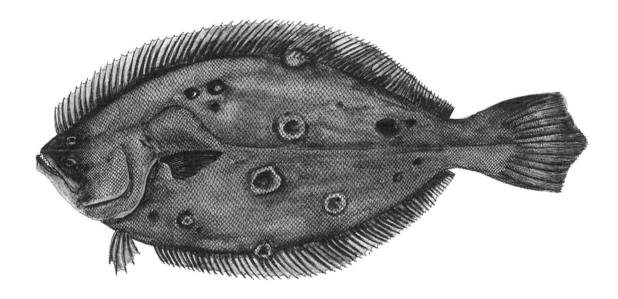

Summer flounder is the largest flounder. It is also known as **fluke** and is found in the Atlantic Ocean. Its brown or grey body is flecked with darker mottles and reaches an average weight of 15 pounds. There is also a **winter flounder**, which is very similar in appearance, although the mottles are less pronounced.

American Plaice

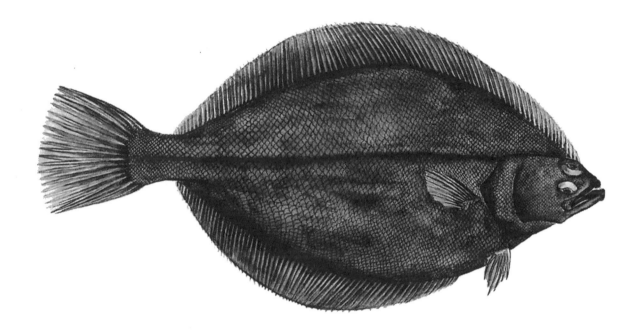

American plaice is the most common sole/flounder in Canada's Atlantic. It is also the most commercially important. Like the other smaller flounders, it has a rounded tail, a greyish upperside and a white underbelly. It reaches an average length of 15 inches, weighing in at close to 3 pounds.

Turbot

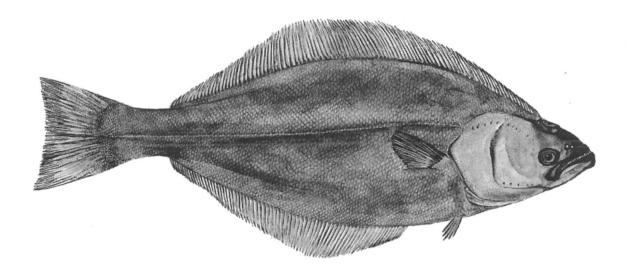

Turbot, also known as **Greenland halibut** and also a member of the sole/flounder grouping of fish, closely resembles the Atlantic halibut. Its weight ranges from 10 to 25 pounds. The turbot is yellowish to greyish brown, and its flesh is denser than that of the Atlantic and Pacific halibuts.

Pacific Ocean Perch

Redfish is almost always commercially known as **ocean perch**, even though it is a member of the **rockfish**, not the perch, family. (The name probably came about because the fish looks similar to **yellow perch**, a freshwater species.) Popular and adaptable in a variety of usually frozen forms, the medium-fat fish is found in the Gulf of St. Lawrence and along the continental shelf from Labrador to Maine. Redfish is a close kin of **Pacific ocean perch**, which is also a rockfish, not a perch, and is the most important of the west coast rockfishes harvested for market.

Yellow Perch

Yellow perch is widely sold fresh or frozen as whole-dressed fish. The average length of a perch is 8 inches, weighing in at 3 to 5 pounds. A cinch for even amateur anglers to catch in lakes, ponds and streams throughout the year, the little, lean, sweet-tasting fish is often called "panfish" because it is tailor-made for a hot frying pan. This fish is found around the world, but there is little doubt that Canada's cool inland waters produce the best flavoured perch anywhere.

Atlantic Cod

Cod is the world's most important commercial food fish. It has been dubbed both "the king of the sea" and "the beef of the sea." In years past, salt and dried cod were the mainstay of the fishing industry. **Atlantic cod** is caught during most of the year. It weighs in at an average of 5 pounds and is available in many forms: fresh, smoked, cured, canned and frozen.

Pacific Cod

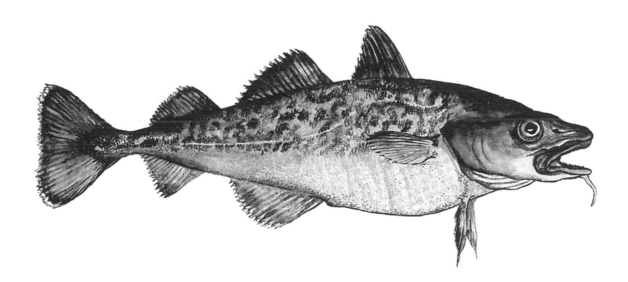

Pacific cod is also known as **grey** or **true cod**. It is found along the entire west coast of Canada throughout the year. Pacific cod reaches, on average, lengths of 20 to 25 inches and weights of 8 to 9 pounds. A cod weighing less than 3 pounds is sometimes called a **scrod**. This versatile fish is suited to any cooking method, and it can replace other lean white fish as well.

Lingcod

Lingcod is not actually a true cod but a greenling. It is also known by several other names, including **buffalo cod** and **leopard cod**. Lingcod is more slender than true cod, reaching an average length of just over 3 feet and a weight of 10 to 11 pounds. It is found on the Pacific coast of Canada.

Haddock

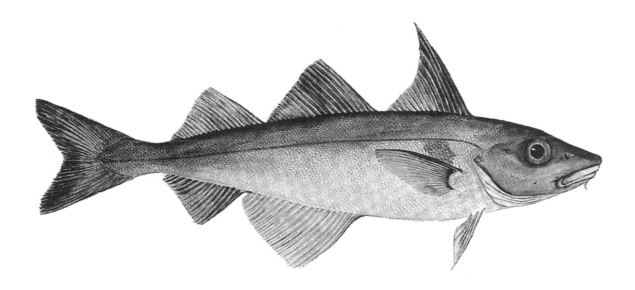

Haddock is a close relative of the cod, which it resembles in both appearance and taste. However, haddock is smaller in size (15 to 25 inches, weighing from 2 to 4 pounds), and its lean flesh is softer in texture. The head and back are dark purple-grey, and the underside is silver-grey. It is harvested all year round, but principally in March.

Pacific Halibut

Pacific halibut is found on the West Coast from California north. Its average weight is 35 pounds, and it is caught commercially from May to November. It is available whole, cut into steaks or boned and filleted, in which case it is known as "fletches."

Atlantic Halibut

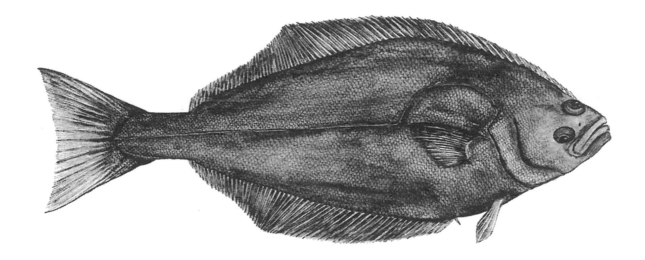

Atlantic halibut can weigh as much as 650 pounds; however, it generally weighs from 5 to 120 pounds. It is the priciest of the flat fishes and can be bought fresh or frozen, whole, cut into steaks or filleted. The meat is white and delicate in flavour.

Atlantic Mackerel

    Mackerel, a pint-sized (with an average weight of 2 pounds) distant relative of the whopping tuna, is more prized as a food fish by Europeans than by North Americans. Of the 60-some mackerel varieties that inhabit the open sea, the three most common are **Atlantic mackerel**, **Spanish mackerel** and **King mackerel**, which is often marketed as **kingfish**. Mackerel flesh is usually darker in colour and oilier than most other fish. Available in a variety of forms, it is especially suitable for broiling and is excellent smoked.

Bluefin Tuna

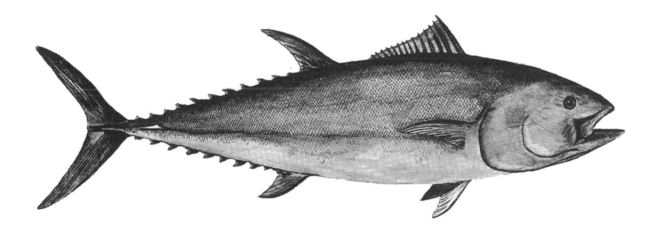

Tuna is, of course, best known as a canned product. Members of the **mackerel** family, tunas range in size from 4-pound small fry to giants exceeding 1,000 pounds. The largest of all tunas is the **bluefin**, which is caught in the Atlantic Ocean off Canada during the late summer and fall. Fresh bluefin tuna is becoming more and more available on the market, usually as steaks or large chunks ready to be baked, broiled, poached or barbecued. **Albacore**, which generally stays in the warm waters of the Atlantic and Pacific, is nearly always the only tuna allowed to bear the prestigious label "white meat" on cans. Bluefin, like **shipjack** and **yellowfin** tuna, must bear the "light meat" label. Canned tuna and canned salmon are usually interchangeable in recipes, while fresh or frozen tuna can often be substituted for such other fish as mackerel, swordfish and shark.

Monkfish

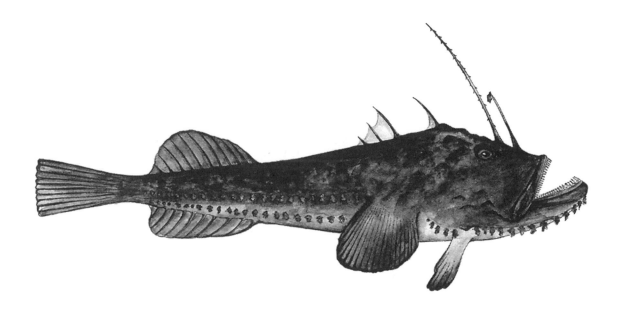

Monkfish — a.k.a. **anglerfish**, **goosefish**, **allmouth** and **bellyfish** — is a stunningly ugly creature that tastes extraordinarily good. Because of its sweet flavour and succulent texture, monkfish has been dubbed "poor man's lobster." The largest monkfish on record weighed in at 60 pounds. Usually marketed as fillets and steaks, monkfish can be used in any recipe that calls for white, firm fish or scallops; it is also very good in bouillabaisse and quenelles. In France, the species is known as **lotte**, a name sometimes used in Canada as well.

Lumpfish

Lumpfish is most noted in Canada for its roe, although it has long been a popular food fish in Europe. Its oval, flattish body is covered with small, round lumps — hence its name. Its pelvic fins form an adhesive disc that allows the lumpfish to sit birdlike on the ocean floor. It is found on the Atlantic coast, primarily off Newfoundland. A female produces an average of 140,000 eggs.

Skate

    Skate, a relative of the shark and readily caught in both the Atlantic and Pacific oceans, is a weird-looking, scaleless fish whose shape resembles a child's kite. Skate "wings" contain firm, white flesh that tastes rather like scallops. The unduly neglected fish is unusual among its kind: skate is better to cook and eat after being refrigerated for two or three days than when it is absolutely fresh. A popular dish in France is poached skate with *beurre noir*, a browned-butter and caper sauce.

Swordfish

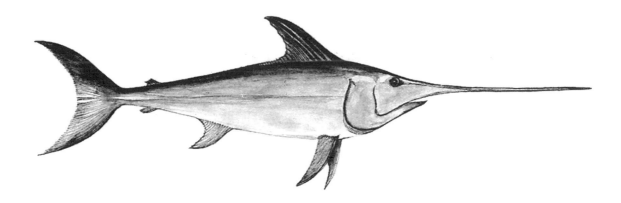

    Swordfish, which swims far and wide in the ocean depths, has become a deservedly popular food fish recently. Also known as **broadbill**, this fish has reached weights as high as 900 pounds and is found on both sides of the Atlantic Ocean. Usually marketed as frozen steaks — though fresh swordfish is often available in the summer and fall — the firm, meaty flesh can be readily baked, broiled or barbecued.

Squid

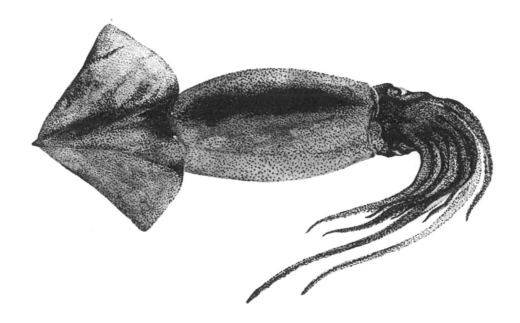

Squid, which is particularly plentiful along Canada's Atlantic coastline, more frequently ends up as bait for fish than as food for people. More's the pity, because the 10-armed mollusc — a relative of the 8-armed **octopus** — is nutritious, versatile, boneless and, last but not least, cheap to buy. Eighty percent of a squid is edible — a remarkably high proportion among aquatic animals. The lean, firm and white flesh can be effectively fried, baked or poached and served hot in sauces or cold in salads. A longtime Mediterranean delicacy, squid is often featured in restaurants as **calamari.**

Pacific Herring

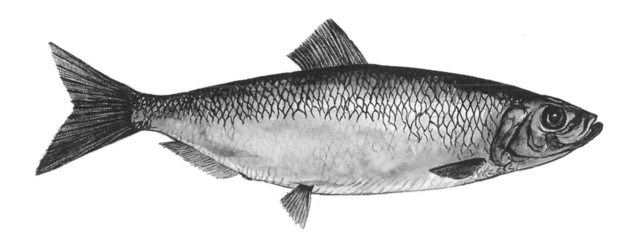

Pacific herring is found throughout the north Pacific Ocean, travelling in huge schools and moving close to shore to breed. Its roe is particularly desirable. Herrings become **kippers** when they are dried and smoked; **bismarck herring** when cured in vinegar, which in turn become **rollmops** when rolled around a pickle. **Sardines** — fresh, frozen or in cans — are any number of small soft-boned members of the extensive herring family.

Herring

Herring, a prolific fat fish of both the Atlantic and Pacific oceans, is much more readily available pickled in delicatessens than fresh in fish markets, although fresh, it lends itself to grilling, pan-frying and baking. Herring has been salted and smoked for centuries.

Lake Herring

Lake herring, or ciscoes, are members of the whitefish family — albeit very small members. Their average weight runs from 1 to 2 pounds. Lake herring are medium-fat fish that can be poached, pan-fried or smoked.

Rainbow Smelt

Rainbow smelt is found in large numbers in the Great Lakes and waterways of southeastern Canada. The bones are edible, and the lean, sweet-tasting smelt is usually pan-fried (after being lightly coated with seasoned flour) or deep-fried.

Capelin

Capelin is found far off the Atlantic coast. It comes inshore to breed along the length of Canada's Atlantic coast, particularly around Newfoundland. It resembles the smelt in coloration but has smaller scales and does not have teeth on its tongue.

Eel

    Eels are found along most of Canada's Atlantic. They have long, thin, snakelike bodies that are darker on top and become lighter down the sides to a white belly. They can reach lengths as great as 4 feet and typically weigh about 15 pounds. Eels breed in salt water, but live most of their lives in fresh water. The meat is available fresh and frozen.

Alewife

Alewife is similiar to herring and, in fact, is sometimes called **river herring**. Much of Canada's alewife fishing is done in the Gasperean River in Acadia. Typical length is around 10 inches. It can best be prepared following herring recipes.

Northern Pike

    Northern pike has been called the wolf of fresh water because it protects its domain with bloody-mindedness. Popular among anglers, the white, firm and finely textured fish is also commercially available fresh or frozen as fillets or whole-dressed. Sometimes called **jackfish**, pike may attain weights of 40 pounds, although the common market weight is from 2 to 5 pounds. Northern pike can be prepared like any other lean fish.

Lake Trout

Trout species are numerous, but they all belong to the salmon family. Many consider **brook trout** the best to eat — especially if it is from the inland waters of Quebec, Labrador or the Maritime Provinces. **Rainbow trout**, a native of the North American Pacific coast, is widely cultivated on fish farms for both home and restaurant markets. **Lake trout**, one of the largest of the freshwater fishes at an average weight of 5 pounds, can be found in deep, cold lakes throughout Canada. Moist and delicate trout flesh ranges in colour from white to pink to bright red. All species can be successfully broiled, pan-fried, baked and poached.

Arctic Char

Arctic char, a native of North American waters, lives primarily in the lakes and streams of countries with Arctic regions. Although found in several countries in the northern hemisphere, Arctic char from Canada is widely considered to be the best in the world. The streamlined body resembles that of a trout or salmon. A delectable fat fish usually marketed whole-dressed or in steak form, Arctic char may be substituted for salmon in most recipes.

Pickerel

Walleye pickerel, or **pike** (or *dore*, in Quebec), is both a sport and a commercial fish. In spite of the name, it belongs to the perch, not the pike, family. ("Walleye" derives from the appearance of the flat eyes, which look as though they are made of glass.) Walleye pickerel, whose average commercial weight is 2 to 4 pounds, is often cooked whole-dressed; the lean, white and firm fillets can be substituted for any other fish fillet in recipes.

Whitefish

   Whitefish — not to be confused with white fish, which could
be any fish with white flesh — are members of the salmon and
trout family. But unlike their relatives, whitefish have con-
sistently white flesh and a rather large flake and delicate taste
when cooked. **Lake whitefish** is caught year-round in lakes
throughout Canada. It is sold in a variety of forms, and its roe is
marketed as "golden caviar." **Tullibee** — often called **lake herring** and known as **cisco** or **chub** in the United States — can be
any one of several small whitefish. While tullibee lends itself best
to pan-frying, lake whitefish may be used in a variety of cooking methods and can be substituted for salmon, trout or flounder
in recipes. Smoked whitefish is widely available.

Mullet

   Mullet is found in the northern freshwater streams and lakes of Canada. It is distinct from the **striped** and **silver mullet** of the United States and the **grey** and **red mullets** of Europe. Canadian mullet is best prepared following recipes for soft white fish as the other mullets have much firmer flesh.

Sea Scallop

    Scallops, of which there are some 400 species worldwide, are Canada's main commercial molluscs; the species **sea scallop** is especially abundant off the Nova Scotia coast. Scallops are bivalves whose edible meat is the interior white muscle that opens and closes the shell. Attached to the muscle is the roe, a delicacy in Europe that is unfortunately seldom marketed in North America. Scallops are graded by size: while sea scallop meat can be as as large as 3 inches, **bay scallops** — *haute cuisine* for gourmets — measure less than 1 inch. Freshly caught scallops, which may be consumed raw, are moist and sweet; fresh or frozen, they can be variously prepared and substituted for other seafood in many recipes.

Dungeness Crab

Crabs are multilegged crustaceans that come in hundreds of varieties, some of which are much more edible than others. Of the large number of varieties inhabiting Canada's Pacific waters, the two most highly prized are **Alaska king crab**, which can weigh up to 20 pounds and is mainly harvested from August through November, and **Dungeness crab**, whose maximum weight is about 4 pounds and is generally caught from May through October. Crab substitutes — sometimes called sea legs or sea shells — are often easier to find on the market today than honest-to-goodness fresh crab. Some substitutes contain 35 percent crab, while others are flavoured products devoid of crab entirely. Most are made from pollack, a plentiful saltwater fish that is subjected to an old Japanese process of fish preservation called *kamaboko*. (This method is also being used to prepare substitutes for shrimp, scallop and lobster.)

Snow Crab

    Snow crab, also known as **queen crab** and **spider crab**, is the most important commercial crab species in Atlantic Canada; its weight averages about 3 pounds and it is principally harvested from June through October and then frozen or canned. The best-known and most widely consumed variety is the **blue crab**, which proliferates from Cape Cod to the Gulf of Mexico and accounts for about half the crab consumed in North America. A **soft-shell crab** is not a separate species, but a blue crab that periodically sheds its shell as it grows. June and July are prime time for soft-shell crabs, which are a treat either sautéed or deep-fried. Whatever the kind, crabmeat has a succulent taste; widely available fresh, frozen or canned, crab can be prepared in a multitude of ways.

Intertidal Hard-Shell Clams

Clams are popular molluscan bivalves whose edible meat is the morsel within the two interconnecting valves or shells. Gathering **soft-shell clams** (or **steamers**) along Atlantic Canada's shoreline at low tide is both a commercial enterprise and a popular sport. These clams can be eaten raw, fried or steamed. A wider variety of clams can be found along the Pacific coast: **butter clams**, the most plentiful, are usually canned or used in chowders; **littleneck clams** and **Manila clams**, which were accidently imported from Japan with Pacific oyster seed in the early 1930s, are often marketed fresh for steaming; **horse clams** are frequently sold minced; and **geoduck clams**, which can reach a weight of 9 pounds, are sometimes cut into steaks for frying.

Pacific Oyster

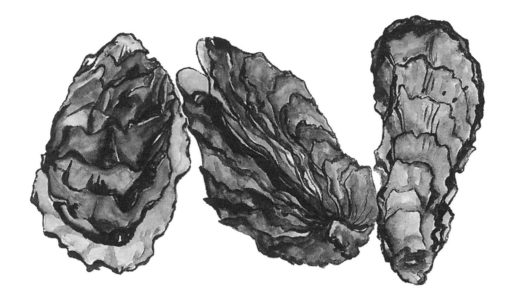

Oysters are such adaptable sea creatures that they now thrive around the world. But the molluscan bivalves living in cold water are generally more desirable than their warm-water counterparts because they grow more slowly. Oysters, which vary in size, colour and flavour depending on their habitat, are identified by the place of origin, hence the names **Malpeque**, **Blue Point**, **Cape Cod**, **Wellfleet**, **Chincoteague**, **Pacific**, and so on. While most oysters in Canada come from the Atlantic region, Pacific oysters, originally imported from Japan in the 1920s, grow in beds throughout British Columbia's Strait of Georgia.

Fall and winter are the best times to eat fresh oysters. In spite of reports to the contrary, they are safe to consume during "r"-less months (May through August), the oyster's breeding season; however, they are watery and insipid compared to the real thing. Oysters can be fried, baked and poached, and cooked in stews, chowders and fritters. They are supreme freshly shucked and eaten on the half shell.

Blue Mussel

Mussels are ubiquitous molluscs that cling to rocks, pebbles, seaweed and whatever along the coastline. The **blue mussel**, particularly prevalent in the Atlantic region, is considered the finest of these tasty bivalves. Many blue mussels, whose smooth shells are blue-black in colour, are cultivated on special farms, especially in Prince Edward Island. Cultivated mussels very often are superior to — and cheaper than — "natural" mussels. A live mussel (the only kind that should ever be cooked and eaten) has its two shells securely closed; when steamed in a heavy pot with a little liquid for about 5 minutes, the shells open and reveal tender, plump, orange-coloured morsels of meat. Eschew Canadian mussels during the summer months when they are skinny and watery.

American Lobster

Lobsters, especially those belonging to the species *Homarus americanus* (American lobster), are probably the most widely esteemed crustaceans in existence. The greatest number of these choice creatures inhabit the coastal waters of Canada's Atlantic provinces. More than half of Canada's lobster catch, which takes place primarily from March through July, is shipped live to the United States, Europe and other parts of Canada. Alive, a 10-legged, two-clawed lobster is greenish black or reddish brown in colour; when cooked, it turns bright red. The usual market weight is 1 to 3 pounds; the edible weight of the rich, firm, juicy meat is about one-third of the live weight. Boiling is the most common method of cooking a whole live lobster: one weighing 1½ pounds — a good size for one person — takes about 15 minutes to cook. Smaller members of the lobster family on the market include **spiny lobster** (commercially known as **rock lobster**), a clawless variety usually imported frozen from Australia or South Africa, and a number of lobsterettes, which are often identified by their place of origin — **Dublin Bay prawns**, **Danish lobster**, **Italian scampi.**

Prawns & Shrimps

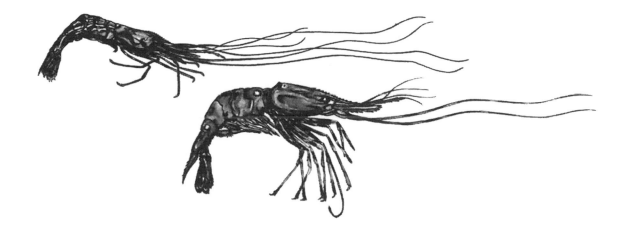

Shrimps rank as Canada's most favoured and often eaten shellfish. The tasty crustaceans are found in both salt water and fresh water as well as on commercial fish farms. Shrimps vary dramatically in size and are marketed according to count and size: while 10 or fewer "colossal" shrimps make 1 pound, it takes as many as 180 "tiny" shrimps to reach the same weight. To get at the edible meat in the delicate shell, the head and the five pairs of legs are removed and the shell is peeled. The intestinal vein — the visible black line on the meat — should also be removed before eating. Although the natural colour of shrimps varies, the meat is a pinkish white when cooked. Shrimp cookery encompasses many methods, and the meat often can be substituted for other shellfish in recipes.

Abalone

Abalone is also known as **Venus' ear**. The foot is the only part of the abalone that is eaten, but it is also collected for its shells. It is found in the Pacific Ocean and is fished commercially mainly in the northern part of British Columbia. It can be bought live or frozen.

How-to

I have laid aside business,
and gone a-fishing.

> — **The Compleat Angler**
> **Izaak Walton**

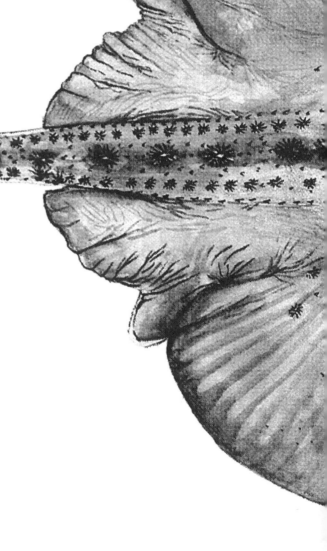

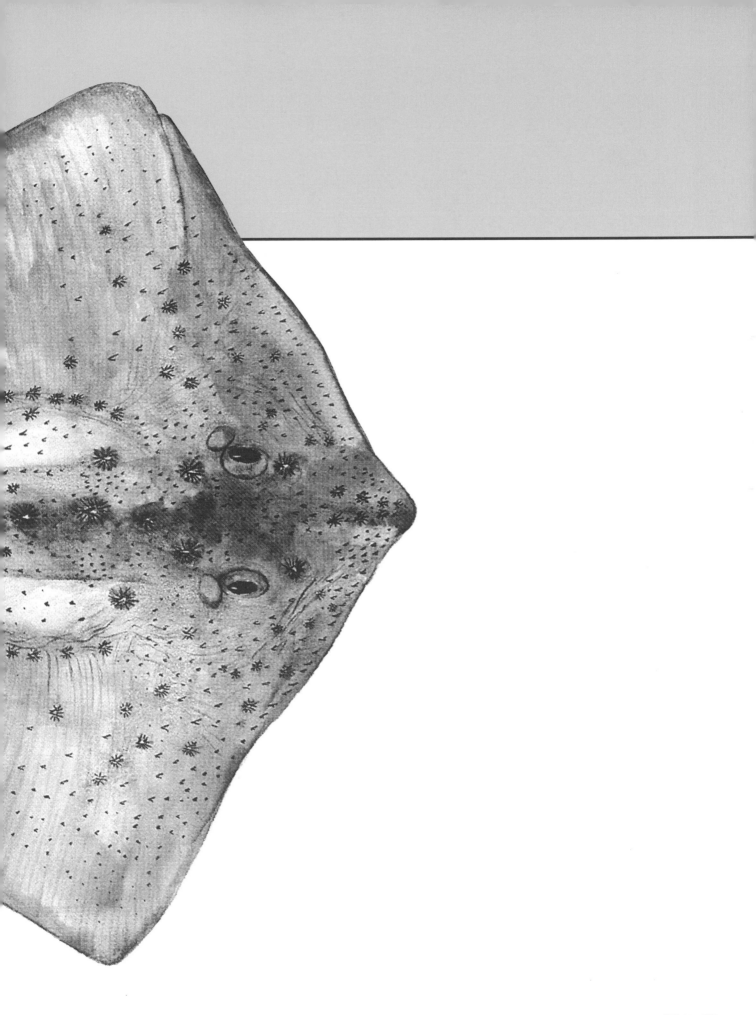

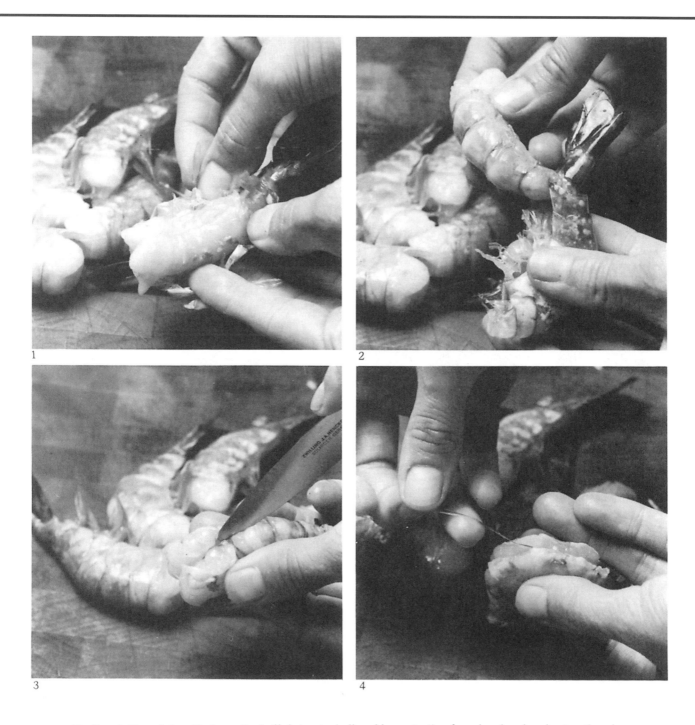

Peeling & Deveining Shrimp: Peel off shrimp's shell and legs, starting from head end and using thumbs, (**1**). Pull shrimp out of shell, tearing gently to separate from tail, (**2**). Slit shrimp down back, (**3**), and lift out intestinal vein (**4**).

Opening an Oyster: It is important to use an oyster knife for this operation. Hold the oyster firmly in one hand with flatter shell up, and insert knife into hinge, (**1**). Twist knife sharply to open shell, (**2**), and then slide knife along inside of upper shell to cut muscle attaching it to flesh. Pull off and discard upper shell, (**3**). Slide knife between muscle and lower shell to separate them from each other, (**4**).

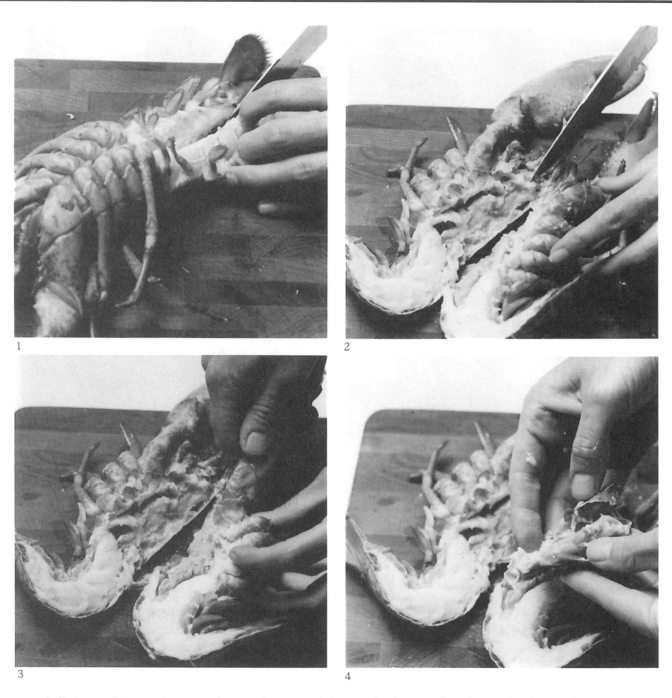

Splitting and Removing Meat from Lobster: Lay lobster on back on work surface with tail toward you. Cut through tail flesh with heavy knife, working back from body and cutting through shell, (**1**). Turn lobster around so tail is away from you, then cut up between legs the length of the body, separating lobster into two, (**2**). Twist off claws at joint between claw and body, (**3**). Remove meat from lower portion of claw, (**4**).

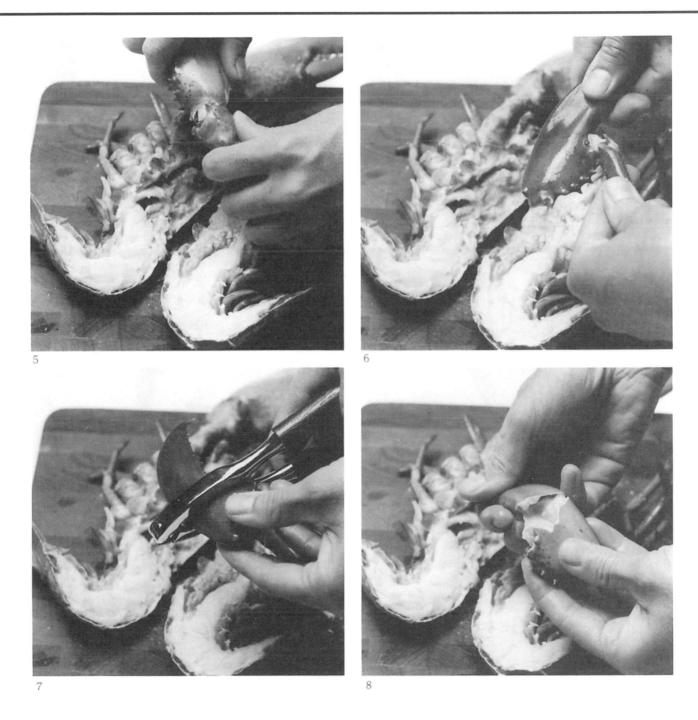

Crack claws at joint, (**5**), pull off pincers, (**6**), and remove meat. Crack main part of claw with lobster cracker (a nutcracker will do the job, too), (**7**), pull apart and remove meat, (**8**). Tail meat can then be removed and eaten.

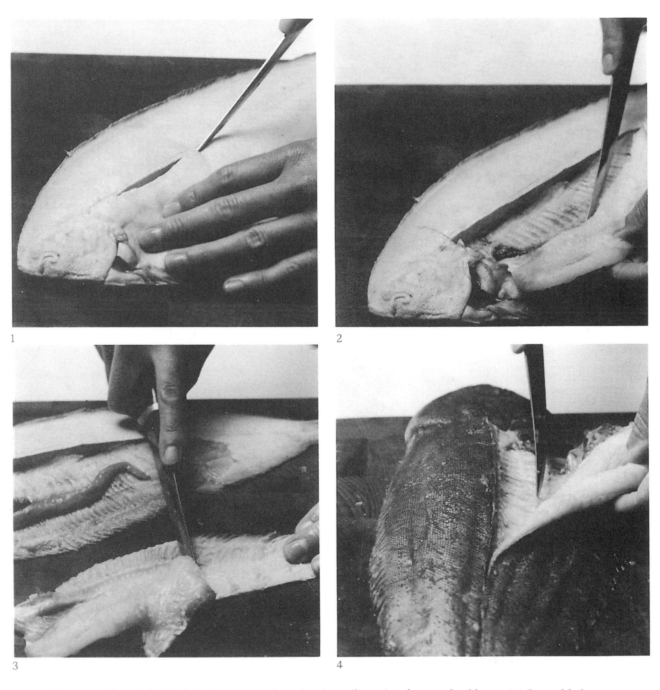

Filleting a Flat Fish: Slit fish along centre from head to tail, cutting down to backbone, (**1**). Insert blade at shallow angle between head end of one fillet and ribs and cut along length of ribs, (**2**). This fillet contains a sac of roe beneath the flesh, (**3**). Cut around this when removing fillets and save to poach or for stock. Once both fillets have been removed from one side of fish, flip and repeat procedure on other side, (**4**).

Filleting a Round Fish: Lay cleaned fish on side and cut along backbone from head to tail, slicing down to expose backbone, (**1**). Insert knife between fillet and ribs and, with knife blade parallel to ribs, cut down length of fillet, (**2**). It will be necessary to use short strokes to detach the flesh completely. Grasp skin firmly with one hand and, using knife to assist, pull away from fillet, (**3**). Some small bones may remain in the fillet; these can be removed using the point of the knife to flip them out, (**4**).

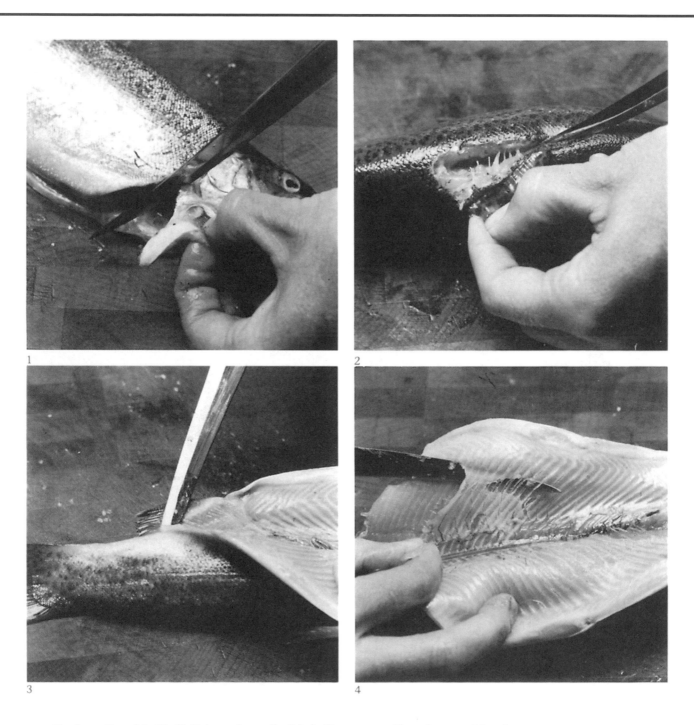

Boning a Trout to Stuff: Using a sharp, flexible knife, remove gills and pectoral fins from just behind the head, (**1**), then carefully cut out dorsal fin, (**2**). Cut belly open to tail, (**3**). Open fish out and separate ribs from flesh, (**4**), working carefully to disturb as little flesh as possible.

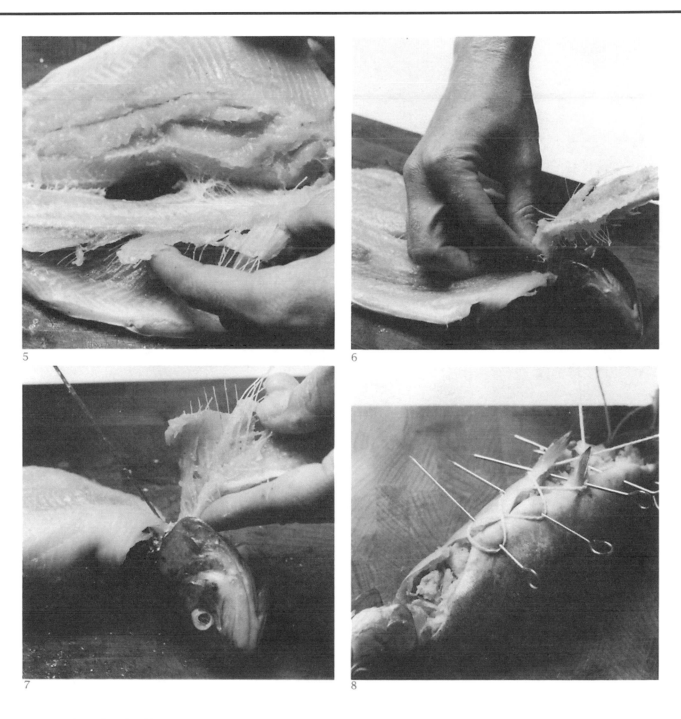

5

6

7

8

Cut through to backbone, so that ribs and backbone can all be separated from flesh, (**5**). Pull skeleton out of fish, working from tail to head, (**6**), cutting through bone at head to separate, (**7**). Once stuffing has been placed in cavity, use skewers to close opening, then lace them shut with string to further secure, (**8**).

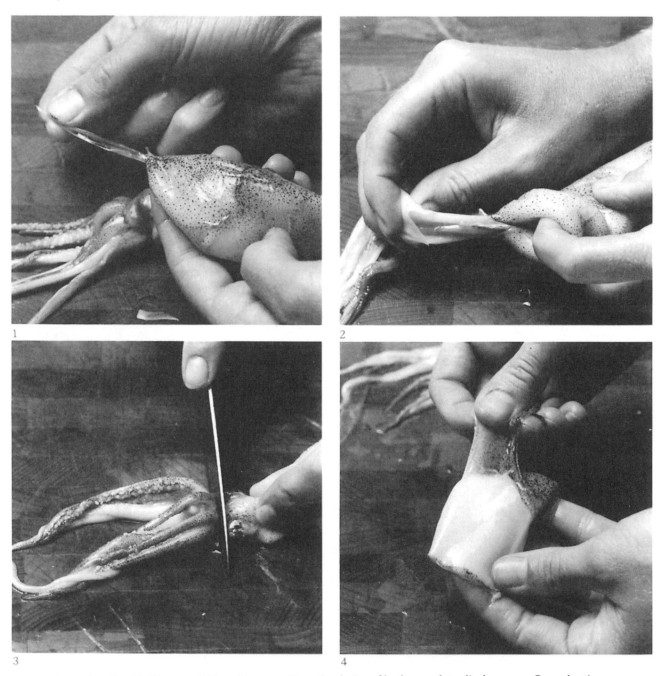

Preparing Squid: Rinse squid in cold water. Draw back rim of body pouch to disclose pen. Grasp by tip, gently pull free, (**1**), and discard. Hold body pouch in one hand and grasp head below eyes with the other. Gently pull the two sections apart, (**2**), thus separating the pouch from the head, tentacles and ink sac. Rinse pouch and pull away lining membrane. Cut off tentacles, slicing just below the eyes, (**3**), and discard head. Skin pouch by slipping a finger under skin and peeling it off, (**4**).

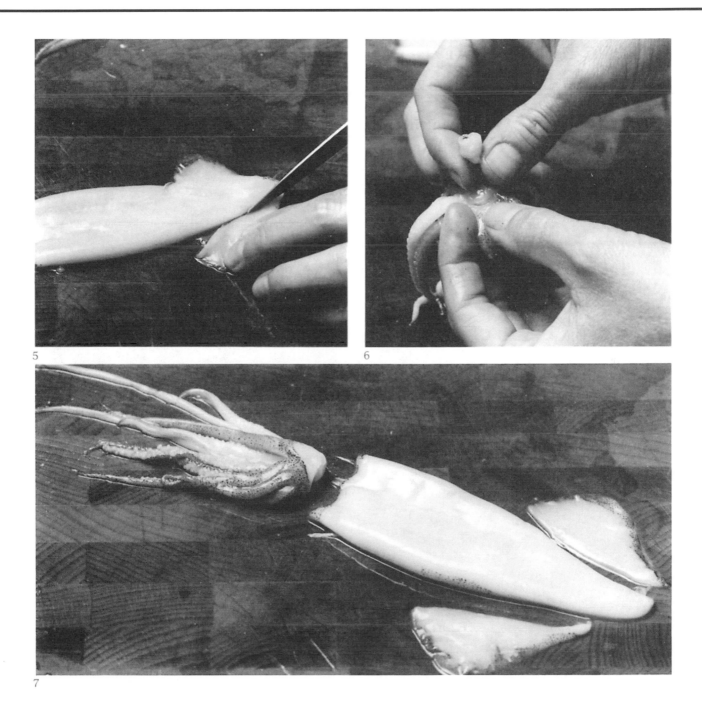

Cut fins from both sides of pouch and skin them, (**5**). The beaklike mouth lies inside the rim of flesh connecting the tentacles. Squeeze this out of rim with fingers and discard, (**6**). The final photograph, (**7**), shows the four edible parts of a squid, ready to cook: the tentacles, the pouch and the fins.

Appetizers

We have here but five
loaves and two fishes.

— St. Matthew 14:17

PISSALADIERE NICOISE

THIS MAKES A DELICIOUS, PIQUANT APPETIZER. SERVED EITHER HOT OR COLD, IT CAN ALSO BE made as individual-sized pizzas.

5 onions
2 cloves garlic, crushed
5 Tbsp. olive oil
½ tsp. salt
⅛ tsp. pepper
½ tsp. basil

½ tsp. thyme
½ tsp. oregano
1 recipe yeast pastry (see page 144)
8 anchovy fillets
16 pitted black olives

Cook onions and garlic slowly in 4 Tbsp. oil with salt until very tender. Sprinkle with pepper, basil, thyme and oregano.

Roll pastry out and place on cookie sheet with a slightly raised rim. Bake at 400 degrees F for 10 minutes. Spread onions on pastry, then arrange anchovy fillets in a fan-shaped design over them. Add olives, placing decoratively among the anchovies. Sprinkle remaining 1 Tbsp. oil over all. Bake at 400 degrees for 10 to 15 minutes or until bubbly.

Serves 4.

— Janet Jokinen
Cobourg, Ontario

SHRIMP WITH YOGURT

THE CONTRIBUTOR RECEIVED THIS RECIPE FROM THE FAMILY SHE LIVED WITH FOR A MONTH IN Sri Lanka, and she cooks it when she wants to conjure up memories of that stay.

2 Tbsp. oil
1 onion, chopped
2 cloves garlic, chopped
1 fresh chili pepper, chopped
1-inch piece ginger, peeled & chopped
2 tomatoes, chopped
1 tsp. coriander seeds
½ tsp. cinnamon

¼ tsp. ground cloves
1 tsp. chili powder
2 tsp. paprika
½ tsp. turmeric
1 tsp. salt
1 lb. shrimp, peeled & deveined
1 cup yogurt

Heat oil in large skillet, then add onion, garlic, chili pepper and ginger. Stir-fry for a few minutes before adding tomatoes, remaining spices and salt. Stir-fry for another minute or so, then add shrimp. Cook until shrimp just turns pink, about 3 minutes, then add ¼ cup yogurt. Cook over high heat until liquid evaporates, turn heat to low and add remaining ¾ cup yogurt. Stir until heated through. Serve over rice.

Serves 4.

— Susan Coulson
Wooler, England

SHRIMP & ARTICHOKE TARTS

2 cups cooked shrimp, drained
1 can artichoke hearts, drained
1 can smoked oysters, drained
2 cups grated Jack cheese
4 green onions, chopped
Pastry for 24 tart shells
1½ cups milk

4 eggs
2 Tbsp. chopped dill weed
Salt & pepper
Paprika
Black olives, sliced
4 Tbsp. Parmesan cheese

Combine shrimp, artichokes, oysters, Jack cheese and onions and place in pastry-lined muffin tins.

Combine milk, eggs, dill, salt and pepper and beat well. Pour over mixture in shells. Top with paprika, olives and Parmesan cheese and bake at 375 degrees F for 20 minutes. Let sit for 10 minutes before serving.

Serves 6 to 8.

— Gillian Barber-Gifford
Rossland, British Columbia

SHRIMP CHEESE SQUARES

GOOD HOT OR COLD, THIS APPETIZER ALSO SERVES WELL AS PICNIC FARE.

Pastry for a two-crust pie
1 Tbsp. butter
1 cup chopped green onions
2 cups grated Swiss cheese
1 lb. cooked shrimp, peeled & deveined
8 eggs

4 cups light cream
2 tsp. fresh dill weed
1 tsp. salt
¼ tsp. pepper
⅛ tsp. cayenne

Roll out pastry to fit a 15½" x 10½" x 1½" jelly-roll pan. Prick all over with a fork. Bake at 425 degrees F for 5 minutes. Cool slightly on a rack. Increase oven temperature to 450 degrees. Melt butter and sauté onions briefly. Sprinkle cheese evenly over pastry, then top with onions and shrimp. In a large bowl, beat eggs, then whisk in cream and seasonings. Pour over pastry shell. Bake for 15 minutes, reduce temperature to 350 degrees and bake until set — about 15 minutes. Cool slightly before cutting into squares.

Makes 32 to 35 squares.

— Holly Andrews
Puslinch, Ontario

ORIENTAL SEAFOOD EGGROLLS

Eggroll Wrappers

IF TIME IS AT A PREMIUM OR YOU ARE CONCERNED ABOUT YOUR ABILITY TO SUCCESSFULLY assemble these wrappers, ready-made wrappers are commercially available.

1 egg
1 cup lukewarm water
1 cup flour
Ginger

¼ cup cornstarch
½ tsp. salt
¼ tsp. almond extract

Beat all ingredients together until smooth. Over low heat, in greased skillet, pour and spread about 2 Tbsp. batter to form a very thin 5-inch-square pancake. Fry on one side for 2 to 3 minutes, removing to a damp cloth before wrappers become brown or crisp. Fill any holes by spreading a bit more batter over them with a pastry brush. Cover with damp cloth until ready to fill.

Filling

3 Tbsp. oil
¼ cup chopped green onions
½ cup finely chopped celery
½ cup diced shrimp, flaked tuna or salmon
½ cup flaked crabmeat, slivered chicken or pork

½ cup chopped water chestnuts
½ cup chopped bean sprouts
¼ cup ground almonds
2 tsp. soya sauce
1 tsp. grated fresh ginger

Oil for deep frying

In a wok or skillet, heat oil, add onions and celery and stir-fry for 3 minutes. Add shrimp and crabmeat and cook for 3 minutes. Add remaining ingredients, then cook for 5 minutes. Cool. Place 2 Tbsp. of mixture down centre of each pancake. Roll up, sealing edge with extra batter or egg. Fry in deep fat at 350 degrees F until golden, or in 1 inch of oil in a skillet.

Makes 10 to 12 eggrolls.

— Helen Shepherd
Lansdowne, Ontario

MUSHROOM AND SHRIMP HORS D'OEUVRES

THIS VERSATILE APPETIZER WAS THE RESULT OF AN EMERGENCY ENTERTAINING SITUATION. More appetizers were needed in a hurry, and there were mushrooms and shrimp left over from other cooking. Any cooked white fish can substitute for the shrimp, herbs can be added, and other fruit juice can be used in place of the lemon juice.

½ cup unsalted butter
2 cloves garlic, minced
Juice of 1 lemon
1 lb. large mushrooms, stems removed
1 medium-sized shrimp for each mushroom,
    cooked, shelled & deveined

Melt butter over low heat, then stir in garlic and lemon juice. Cook over low heat for 1 to 2 minutes. Pour a bit of this mixture into each mushroom cap. Top with a shrimp. If the shrimp are too large to fit into the caps, slice them lengthwise and place each half cut-side down in the cap. Pour more of the butter mixture over the shrimp. Place under the broiler until hot and bubbly.

Serves 6 to 8 as an appetizer.

— Reg Manuel
Sydenham, Ontario

SUI-MUY

ALTHOUGH SOMEWHAT FINICKY TO ASSEMBLE, THESE SHRIMP DUMPLINGS, A TYPICAL CHINESE appetizer, are well worth the effort. The trick is to keep the unused wrappers covered with a damp cloth so they remain soft and easy to work with. Work slowly, and after a few dumplings, you will have mastered the skill.

1 lb. shrimp
¼ lb. ground pork or 1 Tbsp. oil
¾ cup finely chopped celery or Chinese cabbage
½ tsp. salt
¾ cup finely chopped water chestnuts
2 slices ginger, peeled & minced
1 scallion, finely chopped
2 Tbsp. light soya sauce
2 Tbsp. dry sherry
Black pepper
1 Tbsp. sesame oil
1 Tbsp. cornstarch dissolved in 1 Tbsp. water
1 pkg. sui-muy wrappers (substitute wonton
    wrappers if not available)

Shell, devein and coarsely chop shrimp and combine with pork. Combine celery or cabbage with salt and let sit for 5 minutes, squeeze lightly, dry and add to shrimp mixture with remaining ingredients except wrappers. Stir until smooth.

Take the wrappers and pinch pleat about half of each one into 5 small, overlapping pleats, creating a shell with a gathered top and a flat bottom. Hold it in the palm of your hand, and push in 1 tsp. filling with the back of a spoon. Fold the bottom edge to the pleated top and pinch together firmly into a half-moon shape. As you work, keep both wrappers and filled dumplings covered with a damp cloth.

Place dumplings in a bamboo steamer over a pan of water, and steam for 20 minutes over medium-high heat. Serve with light soya sauce sprinkled with ginger.

Serves 6 to 8.

— Carolyn Wells
Kingston, Ontario

PROFITEROLES AUX CREVETTES A L'INDIENNE

PROFITEROLES, OR CREAM PUFFS, CAN FILL MANY ROLES. HERE, THEY ARE TEAMED WITH A curried shrimp filling for a tasty appetizer.

½ cup butter
1 cup water
Salt
1 cup flour
4 eggs
¾ lb. shrimp

1 Tbsp. butter
3 Tbsp. chopped onion
1 Tbsp. curry powder
1 cup heavy cream
3 Tbsp. chutney
Salt & pepper

Place ½ cup butter, water and salt to taste in saucepan. Bring to a boil, then add the flour all at once. Stir constantly until a ball forms and the mixture pulls away from the sides of the pan. Remove from heat and add the eggs one at a time, beating well after each addition.

Butter and flour a baking sheet. Drop the batter from a spoon to form 24 mounds, spacing them well. Bake at 425 degrees F for 30 minutes or until golden brown. Remove from sheet and cool, then slice the top off each puff and remove any soft dough remaining inside.

Meanwhile, cut the shrimp into ½-inch pieces and set aside. Melt the 1 Tbsp. butter and add onion. Cook gently until tender, then stir in curry powder. Add cream and chutney and cook until reduced to approximately ½ cup. Add salt and pepper to taste. Stir in shrimp and cook until they change colour — 5 to 10 minutes.

Spoon curry mixture into cream puff bottoms and replace the tops.

Makes 24 appetizers.

— Heather Quiney
Victoria, British Columbia

COQUILLES ST. JACQUES

ALTHOUGH THIS NAME HAS COME TO BE ASSOCIATED WITH THIS PARTICULAR METHOD OF preparation, Coquilles St. Jacques actually refers to the scallops themselves, which were first popularized when eaten as penance by pilgrims to the shrine of St. James of Compostella.

1 onion, diced
2 Tbsp. butter
½ lb. mushrooms, sliced
¾ lb. scallops
1 cup small shrimp
¾ cup dry white wine
¼ cup butter

¼ cup flour
Salt & pepper
½ tsp. marjoram
1 Tbsp. chopped parsley
1 cup whipping cream
1½ cups mashed potatoes
¼ cup Parmesan cheese

Sauté onion in 2 Tbsp. butter until soft. Add mushrooms, scallops, shrimp and wine. Simmer for 10 minutes. Remove from heat and drain, reserving liquid. Melt ¼ cup butter, stir in flour and cook for one minute, then add cream, the reserved liquid and seasonings. Cook over low heat to make a medium-thick sauce. Add scallop mixture to sauce and heat through. Spoon mixture into individual scallop shells. Pipe mashed potatoes around edges and sprinkle with Parmesan cheese. Heat under broiler until potatoes are lightly browned.

Serves 8.

— Eileen Whitney
Hay Bay, Ontario

ANGELS ON HORSEBACK

A CLASSIC OYSTER RECIPE, THIS IS QUICKLY AND EASILY PREPARED AND PROVIDES A DELICIOUS appetizer.

12 oysters, shucked & rinsed
Flour
Salt & pepper
12 strips bacon, fried until almost crisp

Dust oysters with flour and salt and pepper. Wrap bacon strip around each oyster and hold together with a toothpick. Broil for 4 to 6 minutes, or until bacon is crisp.

Serves 3.

— Nina Christmas
Courtenay, British Columbia

FRESH OYSTERS IN SPINACH LEAVES

12 large spinach or chard leaves
1 egg yolk
½ tsp. Dijon mustard
White pepper

½ cup peanut oil
24 fresh oysters, juice & deeper half
  of each shell reserved
½ tsp. paprika

Steam spinach or chard leaves until tender but still bright green — about 2 minutes. Rinse under cold water and pat dry. Cut each leaf lengthwise along both sides of the centre rib to divide the leaves in half.

Whisk egg yolk with mustard and pepper until thickened. Gradually whisk in the oil in a thin stream to make a thick mayonnaise.

Strain the reserved oyster juice through a fine sieve lined with dampened cheesecloth. Bring to a boil in a saucepan and boil until reduced by half — about 4 minutes. Remove from heat and let cool to room temperature. Whisk into the mayonnaise.

Wrap each oyster in a spinach or chard leaf and place seamside down on a half shell. Spoon 1 tablespoon of mayonnaise over the middle of each oyster, leaving some of the spinach or chard exposed for colour contrast. Sprinkle lightly with paprika.

Bake at 350 degrees F for 15 minutes.

Serves 4.

— Lucia M. Cyre
Logan Lake, British Columbia

MUSSELS PROVENCALE

¼ cup olive oil
3 cloves garlic, finely chopped
2 onions, chopped
1 stalk celery, chopped
1 28-oz. can tomatoes, drained,
  or 2 lbs. tomatoes, peeled,
  cored & chopped

1 7-oz. can tomato paste
1 cup red or white wine
¼ cup loosely packed, chopped basil,
  or 2 tsp. dried
Salt & pepper
24 mussels

In heavy, lidded saucepan, heat oil, then sauté garlic, onion and celery until soft but not brown. Add tomatoes and simmer for 10 minutes to evaporate remaining liquid. Add remaining ingredients except mussels and simmer for 30 minutes.

Just before serving, add scrubbed mussels. Cover and simmer for 3 to 5 minutes or until mussels open.

Serves 4 as an appetizer, 2 as a main course.

— M.J. Wass
Kingston, Ontario

TUNA TEASERS

THIS IS AN EASY-TO-MAKE APPETIZER, WHICH CAN ALSO BE SERVED WITH SOUP AND A SALAD FOR a complete meal.

1 cup flour
1½ tsp. baking powder
1 tsp. onion salt
½ tsp. curry powder
¼ cup butter

7-oz. can tuna, drained & flaked
1 cup grated Cheddar cheese
1 Tbsp. finely minced green pepper
½ cup milk

Combine flour, baking powder, onion salt and curry powder in a mixing bowl. Cut in butter until it is the size of small peas. Add tuna, cheese and green pepper. Add milk all at once and blend well.

Drop by teaspoonfuls onto lightly greased cookie sheet and bake at 450 degrees F for 12 to 15 minutes.

Makes about 18.

— *Mary E. Bailey*
Lethbridge, Alberta

GRAVLAX

THIS IS A POPULAR SCANDINAVIAN APPETIZER WHICH IS MADE WITH FRESH SALMON, ALTHOUGH the contributor has used frozen salmon as well as Arctic char with good results. Serve chilled with lots of thinly sliced rye bread that has been lightly buttered.

1 Tbsp. pickling salt
1 Tbsp. sugar
1 tsp. crushed peppercorns
1 Tbsp. fresh dill weed or ½ tsp. dried
1 lb. salmon fillets, boned
2 tsp. Cognac
Gravlax Sauce (recipe follows)

Mix salt, sugar, pepper and dill and sprinkle over fillets, rubbing in well. Sprinkle with Cognac. Wrap fillets in foil, making sure that juices are sealed. Store in refrigerator for 3 to 4 days, weighting it down with a heavy board. Turn once a day.

To serve, clean excess spices from each fillet. Slice very thinly on the diagonal. Serve with Gravlax Sauce and rye bread.

Serves 8.

— *Judy Koster*
Bridgewater, Nova Scotia

GRAVLAX SAUCE

3 Tbsp. oil
1 Tbsp. red wine vinegar
1 Tbsp. sugar
2 to 3 Tbsp. Dijon or Pommery mustard
Salt & white pepper
2 to 3 Tbsp. fresh dill

Combine all ingredients except dill and mix well. Stir in dill or serve it separately.

Makes enough sauce for 1 lb. Gravlax, which will serve 8 people.

— *Judy Koster*
Bridgewater, Nova Scotia

ESCABECHE

2 lbs. halibut, turbot, sole or red snapper
¼ cup olive oil
2 medium onions, thinly sliced
1 large clove garlic, minced
2 carrots, peeled & thinly sliced
Pepper
¾ cup white wine vinegar
2 cinnamon sticks, broken
¼ cup dry white wine
¼ cup water
1 tsp. salt
¼ tsp. coriander seeds
2 bay leaves
1 small lime, sliced
Stuffed olives

Rinse fish and pat dry. Heat oil in large skillet and sauté fish until light brown — about 2 minutes on each side. Remove to glass baking dish, leaving oil in skillet.

Sauté onions, garlic and carrots in skillet for 2 minutes, adding oil if necessary. Stir in pepper to taste and cook for 1 minute. Stir in remaining ingredients except for fish, lime and olives. Bring to a boil, reduce heat and simmer for 1 minute.

Pour vegetable mixture over fish, cool, then refrigerate for at least 24 hours. Garnish with lime slices and olives and serve.

Serves 4.

— *Jacline Limoges*
Warren, Ontario

LOBSTER IN SUGAR SNAPS

½ lb. cooked & chopped lobster
2 Tbsp. mayonnaise
¼ tsp. dried dill weed
3-4 drops Tabasco sauce
Lemon juice
30 sugar snap peas

Combine lobster, mayonnaise, dill weed, Tabasco sauce and lemon juice and mix well.

Working carefully, open the peas to form an envelope. Stuff with lobster mixture. Refrigerate for a few hours.

Serves 6.

— *Louise McDonald*
L'Orignal, Ontario

HERRING IN CREAM SAUCE

THIS IS JUST ONE OF THE MANY WAYS HERRING CAN BE PREPARED TO BE SERVED AS PART OF THE first course of a traditional Swedish smorgasbord.

8-12 oz. pickled cut herring
¼ cup mayonnaise
2 Tbsp. whipping cream
¼ tsp. sugar
⅛ tsp. lemon pepper
⅛ tsp. Worcestershire sauce
½ cup chopped red onion
½ cup leeks, cut into rings
1 cup dill weed
Pepper

Drain herring, reserving 1 Tbsp. of the marinade. Combine mayonnaise, whipping cream, sugar, lemon pepper, Worcestershire sauce and the reserved marinade.

Arrange half the onions, half the leeks and half the dill on serving plate. Sprinkle with pepper and place herring on top. Top with remaining onions, leeks and dill. Spread mayonnaise mixture over all, garnish with dill and refrigerate until thoroughly chilled.

Serves 8.

— *Laurabel Miller*
Denbigh, Ontario

SWEET HERRING

2 large mild white onions, thinly sliced into rings
   & separated
Salt
16-oz. jar herring in wine sauce
2 large green apples
1 cup sour cream
1 Tbsp. dill weed
1 tsp. salt

Place onions in colander and liberally sprinkle with salt. Slowly pour about 1 quart boiling water over onions, rinse well with cold water and let drain. Dry well.

Drain herring into bowl, discarding liquid. Peel, core and dice apples. Add sour cream, sliced onion, dill, apple and salt to herring and mix gently but thoroughly.

Serves 4 to 6.

— *Judi Knapfl*
Coquitlam, British Columbia

FISH IN LEMON ASPIC

2 Tbsp. unflavoured gelatin
¼ cup cold water
1½ cups hot water
½ tsp. salt
1 Tbsp. sugar
½ cup freshly squeezed lemon juice

1 cup cooked, flaked fish
2 Tbsp. chopped pimento
1 cup chopped celery
6-8 lettuce leaves
Mayonnaise to garnish

Soften gelatin in cold water. Add hot water, salt, sugar and lemon juice. Chill until partially set. Stir in fish, pimento and celery. Spoon into individual moulds. Chill for several hours before serving on lettuce leaves with mayonnaise.

Serves 6 to 8.

— *Carol A. Smith*
Whitehorse, Yukon

SALMON CREAM CHEESE APPETIZER

THIS IS AN ATTEMPT TO DUPLICATE AN APPETIZER THE CONTRIBUTOR HAD AT A CATERED PARTY. It should be very smooth and is excellent served on crackers.

8 oz. cream cheese, softened
7-oz. can salmon, drained
2 Tbsp. chopped green onion
2 Tbsp. chopped parsley

Tabasco sauce
Worcestershire sauce
Finely chopped walnuts
Fresh parsley sprigs

Combine all ingredients except nuts and parsley sprigs. Form into desired shape and chill thoroughly. Just before serving, press walnuts on top and sides. Garnish with fresh parsley.

Serves 6 to 8.

— *Wendy Vine*
Ganges, British Columbia

SMOKED SALMON ROLLS

1 tsp. lemon juice
Freshly ground pepper
1 tsp. dill weed or 1 Tbsp. chopped
   capers
¼ lb. cream cheese, softened
½ lb. smoked salmon, cut in slices
Parsley

Mix seasonings into cream cheese. Spread over smoked salmon slices. Roll each slice up and chill well. To serve, slice each roll into ½-inch rounds. Serve on crackers, sprinkled with parsley.

Serves 4 to 6.

— Randi Kennedy
Stella, Ontario

CANADIAN SMOKED SALMON

1 lb. smoked salmon
Juice of 1 lemon
2 Tbsp. mayonnaise
1 dill pickle, finely chopped
1 large green onion, finely chopped

Salt & pepper
Salad greens
Tomato, radishes, cucumbers &
   green peppers to garnish

Slice salmon thinly, removing bones and skin. This is most easily done if the salmon has been placed in the freezer for a few hours first.

Toss in lemon juice and mayonnaise. Add dill pickle, onion, salt and pepper. Toss again and refrigerate.

Serve on a bed of greens, garnished with raw vegetables.

Serves 6 as an appetizer.

— Nita Hunton
Cambridge, Ontario

MARINATED SHRIMP AND MUSHROOMS

1 lb. shrimp, cooked, shelled & deveined
3 cups small fresh mushroom caps
1 onion, sliced into rings
2 Tbsp. chopped parsley
½ green pepper, sliced into thin strips
½ sweet red pepper, sliced into thin strips
3 cloves garlic, chopped

1½ cups white wine vinegar
½ cup water
⅓ cup olive oil
1 Tbsp. pickling spice
Salt
Lettuce & lemon twists to garnish

In a shallow bowl, combine shrimp, mushroom caps, onion, parsley and peppers. In a saucepan, combine remaining ingredients except for garnish and simmer for 5 minutes. Pour marinade over shrimp mixture, cover and refrigerate overnight. Serve on lettuce with lemon twists.

Serves 6.

— Judy Koster
Bridgewater, Nova Scotia

SOLE MOUSSE

½ cup water
¼ cup dry sherry
1 lb. sole fillets
¼ cup cold water
1 Tbsp. unflavoured gelatin

½ tsp. salt
7½-oz. can salmon, or 1 cup cooked salmon
½ cup minced watercress
1 cup whipping cream

Bring water and sherry to a boil in a saucepan. Add sole fillets, cover and cook over medium heat until fish flakes easily with a fork — about 15 minutes. Remove fish and set aside. Reserve ½ cup of the poaching liquid.

Place ¼ cup cold water in a small saucepan, sprinkle with gelatin and let stand for 1 minute to soften. Add reserved poaching liquid, then heat gently until gelatin is completely dissolved.

Combine sole, gelatin mixture and salt in a blender. Blend until very smooth. Place in a bowl, cover and refrigerate for 45 minutes or until nearly set.

In a second bowl, flake salmon. Place minced watercress in a third bowl. Beat whipping cream until soft peaks form, then fold into sole mixture, blending well. Add ½ cup of this mixture to salmon. Fold ½ cup into watercress. Spoon one half of remaining sole mixture into a lightly oiled 9-by-5-inch loaf pan. Spread salmon mixture over sole, then spread watercress mixture over salmon. Spoon remaining sole mixture on top. Cover and refrigerate until firm.

Serve, sliced, with Caper Mayonnaise (recipe follows).

Serves 6 to 8.

— *Janet Jokinen*
Cobourg, Ontario

CAPER MAYONNAISE

1 cup mayonnaise
¼ cup milk
2 Tbsp. lemon juice
2 Tbsp. minced capers

Combine all ingredients until well blended.

— *Janet Jokinen*
Cobourg, Ontario

CRAB AND CUCUMBER MOUSSE

1 Tbsp. unflavoured gelatin
1 cup milk
1 cup sour cream
2 Tbsp. lemon juice
½ tsp. dill weed
½ tsp. salt

White pepper
½ cup peeled, seeded & diced cucumber
2 Tbsp. minced onion
1 cup cottage cheese
½ lb. crabmeat, drained

Soften gelatin in milk, then heat until completely dissolved. Cool. Combine sour cream, lemon juice and seasonings. Stir into milk. Chill until slightly thickened. In blender, purée cucumber, onion, cottage cheese and crabmeat. Fold into milk. Pour into greased 1-quart mould. Chill until firm.

Serves 6 to 8.

— *Valerie Marien*
Orangeville, Ontario

CURRIED TUNA MOUSSE

3¼-oz. can chunk light tuna, undrained
½-¾ cup chicken stock
1 Tbsp. unflavoured gelatin
¼ cup mayonnaise
½ cup cream cheese, softened

½ celery stalk, coarsely chopped
Slice of onion
1 Tbsp. chopped parsley
½ tsp. curry powder
⅛ tsp. dry mustard

Drain liquid from tuna into a measuring cup. Add enough chicken stock to make ¾ cup. Pour into a small saucepan and bring to a boil. Place gelatin in blender, add boiling liquid, cover and blend until gelatin is dissolved – about 30 seconds. Add remaining ingredients, cover and blend for about 60 seconds or until smooth. Pour mixture into a lightly greased 2-cup mould. Mousse may be frozen for 30 minutes or refrigerated overnight.

Serves 2.

— Nan Millette
Corunna, Ontario

TAPENADE

This is a traditional Provencale hors d'oeuvre that, in its classic form, calls for many more anchovies and no sardines. Serve as a dip with raw vegetables or spooned over crusty French bread.

7-oz. can tuna with oil
2-oz. can anchovy fillets with oil
3¾-oz. can skinless, boneless sardines with oil
¼ cup capers
2 cloves garlic, crushed
20 ripe olives, pitted

⅓ cup olive oil
¼ tsp. white pepper
⅛ tsp. dry mustard
1 Tbsp. lemon juice
¼ cup Cognac or brandy

Combine tuna, anchovies, sardines, capers, garlic and olives in a bowl. Place about one-third of this mixture in blender at a time and blend until just smooth. Gradually add olive oil to each batch, using one-third each time. When mixture is all blended, stir together in bowl and add pepper, mustard, lemon juice and Cognac, mixing well.

Makes approximately 3 cups.

— Jane Meszaros
Sturgeon Falls, Ontario

CRAB DELIGHT

This appetizer is especially delicious served in avocado halves, topped with alfalfa sprouts.

8 oz. cream cheese, softened
1 Tbsp. milk
6 oz. cooked crabmeat
1 Tbsp. finely chopped green onion
Pinch Dijon mustard
Pinch salt

Cream together cheese and milk until soft and smooth. Add crabmeat, onion, mustard and salt. Blend well.

Refrigerate for 3 to 4 hours. Serve with crackers or bite-sized fresh vegetables.

Serves 4 to 6.

— Brenda Watts
Surrey, British Columbia

KAUAI CRAB SPREAD

8 oz. crabmeat
1 cup sour cream
2 tsp. curry
¼ cup chutney
¼ cup desiccated coconut

Combine all ingredients (draining crab well if canned or frozen is used). Chill.

Serve with crackers as a spread or with raw vegetables as a dip.

Makes 2½ cups.

— Holly Andrews
Puslinch, Ontario

SULA KALA

A FORM OF PICKLED SALMON, THIS CAN BE SERVED WITH RYE BREAD SPREAD WITH CREAM CHEESE and topped with thinly sliced Spanish onion.

10-lb. coho salmon
1½ cups pickling salt
1½ cups brown sugar

Cut salmon in half lengthwise and remove backbone and ribs, but leave skin intact. Rub mixture of salt and brown sugar on fish. Place one half skin side down, in a long dish. Place second half on top with the skin up. Cover with foil, place weight on top and leave in a cool place for 24 hours. Lift fish from mixture, which will have become liquid, and rinse well with cold water. Dry with towel, and when ready to serve, cut into thin slices on the diagonal.

Makes 10 lbs.

— Joann Alho
Brantford, Ontario

CLAM DIP

THIS MAKES A DELICIOUS DIP FOR CRACKERS OR CRUDITES AND EVEN WAS ENJOYED BY SOME OF the contributor's friends who claimed they did not like clam dip.

1 can minced or baby clams
8 oz. cream cheese, softened
2 Tbsp. mayonnaise
2 Tbsp. sour cream
1 tsp. Worcestershire sauce
Dry mustard
1 clove garlic, minced
2 green onions, minced

Drain clams, reserving liquid. Combine all ingredients well. Stir in enough reserved clam juice to give the desired consistency. Refrigerate for at least 2 hours before serving.

Makes 2 cups.

— Cinda Chavich
Saskatoon, Saskatchewan

SMOKED OYSTER DIP

1 can smoked oysters, finely chopped & juice reserved
¾ cup chopped celery
½ cup chopped onion
4 slices crisp bacon, crumbled

8 soda crackers, crumbled
2-3 Tbsp. bacon drippings
2 eggs, hard-boiled & finely chopped
6 Tbsp. mayonnaise
Juice of 1 lemon

Combine all ingredients, mix well and refrigerate for 24 hours. Serve with vegetable sticks and crackers.

Makes approximately 3 cups.

— Cynthia Gilmore
Toronto, Ontario

ANCHOVY DIP

8 oz. cream cheese
1 cup sour cream
1 can anchovies
¼ cup sweet pickled cocktail onions
2 cloves garlic

Cream together cheese and sour cream. Finely mince anchovies, onions and garlic. Stir into cheese mixture. Serve with fresh raw vegetables.

Makes 2 cups.

— Maureen Johnson
Pembroke, Ontario

SPINACH TUNA PATE

Butter
2 lbs. spinach, stemmed & washed
¾ cup whipping cream
3 large eggs
6-oz. can tuna, drained & flaked
½ cup minced scallions
4 anchovy fillets, drained

1 Tbsp. lemon juice
⅓ cup soft white bread crumbs
1 tsp. salt
⅛ tsp. pepper
Lemon wedges
Parsley sprigs

Butter bottom of loaf pan, line with wax paper, and butter paper lightly.

Cook spinach in large saucepan of boiling, salted water until tender — about 3 minutes. Drain in colander and rinse under cold, running water to cool. Squeeze spinach to remove as much moisture as possible, then chop coarsely. Set aside.

Purée cream, eggs, tuna, scallions, anchovies and lemon juice in blender or food processor until smooth. Turn tuna mixture into medium bowl. Add bread crumbs, salt, pepper and spinach and stir to mix well.

Pour spinach mixture into prepared pan and cover with aluminum foil. Place loaf pan in larger baking dish or small roasting pan and fill with boiling water halfway up sides of loaf pan. Bake in centre of oven at 375 degrees F until knife inserted in centre of pâté comes out clean but wet — about 1 hour. Remove from water bath and cool in pan on rack to room temperature. Refrigerate, covered, until chilled — about 3 hours.

At serving time, remove pâté from mould and place on serving platter. Cut into ½-inch slices and garnish with lemon wedges and parsley.

Serves 8 to 12 as an appetizer.

— Erika Maurer
Smithers, British Columbia

SMOKED SALMON PATE

6 oz. smoked salmon, coarsely chopped
2 Tbsp. lemon juice
½ cup butter, melted
½ cup sour cream

1 Tbsp. fresh dill weed
Salt & pepper
Lemon slices
Thinly sliced rye bread

Place salmon and lemon juice in food processor or blender and process until smooth. With machine running, add melted butter in a slow, steady stream. Scrape down container once.

Place salmon mixture in a bowl and stir in sour cream and dill weed. Taste and adjust seasonings, adding salt and pepper if needed.

Refrigerate, covered, for up to 2 days, but serve at room temperature accompanied by lemon slices and rye bread.

Makes 1½ cups.

— Pam Collacott
North Gower, Ontario

SALMON BUTTER

THIS BUTTER IS DELICIOUS ON MELBA TOAST BUT CAN ALSO BE SERVED WITH DELICATELY flavoured fish, such as sole or flounder. It can be kept frozen for 3 months if tightly wrapped in foil.

¼ lb. smoked salmon
½ lb. unsalted butter, softened
1 tsp. chervil
1 Tbsp. lemon juice
Salt & pepper

Grind salmon to a fine paste or process in a food processor until smooth. Blend with remaining ingredients to make a smooth butter.

Makes 2 cups.

— Mrs. L. Murphy
Mississauga, Ontario

MACKEREL PATE

½ lb. smoked mackerel
8 oz. cream cheese, softened
1 Tbsp. minced onion
1 Tbsp. lemon juice
1 Tbsp. prepared horseradish

½ tsp. Worcestershire sauce
½ cup chopped nuts (almonds, walnuts or
   pecans)
2 Tbsp. finely chopped parsley

Remove bones and skin from mackerel and flake with a fork. Combine with cream cheese, onion, lemon juice, horseradish and Worcestershire sauce. Chill for 3 hours. Shape into a log or ball. Roll in a mixture of nuts and parsley. Serve with crackers and crudités.

Makes 2 cups.

— Judy Koster
Bridgewater, Nova Scotia

COD ROE PATE

12 oz. smoked cod roe
1 tsp. onion juice (from grated onion)
½ cup olive oil
1 cup fresh white bread crumbs
¼ lb. cream cheese
Lemon juice
Pepper

Scrape roe from skin and place in bowl with onion juice. Pour oil over bread crumbs and leave to soak for 5 minutes. Mix roe with cheese until smooth, then work in bread crumbs and oil a little at a time. Season with lemon juice and pepper to taste.

Serve with rye crackers, black olives and lemon wedges.

Makes approximately 1½ cups.

— Frances Houkine
Pickering, Ontario

KIPPER PATE

7-oz. pkg. kipper fillets
Juice of 1 lemon
1 clove garlic, crushed
1 cup unsalted butter
Pepper

Combine all ingredients and blend well. Chill for a few hours before serving.

Makes approximately 1½ cups.

— Maureen Evans
Bradford, Ontario

OYSTERS ROCKEFELLER

10 oz. spinach
18-20 oysters in shells
¼ cup butter
½ cup finely chopped onion
2 Tbsp. flour
Milk
2 Tbsp. chopped parsley
1 clove garlic, crushed
⅛ tsp. nutmeg
1 tsp. salt
Pepper
¼ lb. mozzarella cheese, grated
¼ cup fine bread crumbs
2-3 Tbsp. white wine
Rock salt
Parmesan cheese

Lightly steam spinach, drain and set aside. Remove oysters from shells, reserving juice and deeper halves of shells. Wash oysters thoroughly under cold running water.

Melt butter over low heat. Add onion and sauté until tender. Stir in flour and cook for 1 minute. Stir in reserved oyster juice, and add milk, if necessary, to make ½ cup liquid. Add parsley, garlic, nutmeg, salt and pepper. Simmer, stirring, until thickened. Stir well-drained spinach into sauce along with mozzarella cheese and bread crumbs. Stir in wine. Cook, stirring, over medium-low heat for 3 to 4 minutes.

Place a pinch of rock salt in bottom of each reserved shell. Place an oyster on top of salt, then spoon sauce over oysters. Sprinkle with Parmesan cheese, and bake at 400 degrees F for 10 to 12 minutes. Serve immediately.

Serves 4 to 5.

— Diane Rondeau
Thunder Bay, Ontario

WHISTLING OYSTERS

8 Tbsp. unsalted butter
1 cup fine, soft bread crumbs
2 Tbsp. minced parsley
2 cloves garlic, minced
3 Tbsp. chopped herbs (dill, basil,
 tarragon & chervil)

¼ tsp. salt
¼ tsp. white pepper
24 fresh oysters, shucked, with juice
 reserved
½ cup heavy cream
Chopped parsley & lemon wedges
 to garnish

Melt 4 Tbsp. butter. Add bread crumbs, parsley and garlic, stirring to blend. Remove from heat and set aside.

Blend chopped herbs with remaining 4 Tbsp. butter and salt and pepper in small bowl.

Sprinkle half the bread-crumb mixture over the bottoms of four au gratin dishes. Place 6 oysters in each dish, and spoon oyster juice equally over them. Dot with herb butter, and top with remaining bread crumbs. Spoon 2 Tbsp. cream over each dish.

Bake at 375 degrees F for 15 minutes, or until mixture is bubbly and golden brown. Garnish and serve.

Serves 4.

— *Lucia Cyre*
Logan Lake, British Columbia

SOUSED MACKEREL

2 lbs. mackerel, cleaned & boned (any oily fish
 can be used)
1 medium onion, coarsely chopped
1 cup dry white wine
2 bay leaves

½ cup white wine vinegar
1 cup water
1 tsp. demerara sugar
2 tsp. salt
6 peppercorns

Wash fish. Place skin side up in a shallow pan. Combine remaining ingredients and bring to a boil. Pour over fish. Cover, then bake at 350 degrees F for 10 minutes. Let fish cool in the marinade overnight. Serve cold with sour pickles, capers, sour cream and lots of fresh bread.

Makes approximately 6 cups.

— *Melville Luke*
Outlook, Saskatchewan

PICKLED FISH

2 lbs. firm white fish (swordfish is excellent)
½ cup oil
4 large onions, chopped
1 tsp. turmeric
2 tsp. curry powder
1½ cups vinegar
Salt

Cut fish into 2- to 3-inch pieces. Fry in oil until cooked through. Combine remaining ingredients in a saucepan. Bring to a boil then simmer until onions are tender. In a glass jar, arrange alternate layers of fish and onion mixture. Refrigerate overnight then serve cold. This will keep for 2 weeks in a glass jar if refrigerated.

Makes approximately 6 cups.

— *Lucille Schur*
Toronto, Ontario

MCKENNA'S SCALLOP SEVICHE

1 lb. scallops
½ cup lemon juice
½ cup lime juice
¼ cup olive oil
½ tsp. salt
Pepper
1-2 fresh hot peppers, seeded
  & chopped

1 clove garlic, minced
2 tomatoes, chopped
3-4 scallions, chopped
1 green pepper, chopped
1-2 Tbsp. minced fresh coriander
Lettuce leaves

Rinse scallops under cold water and drain. If they are very large, halve them.

Combine lemon and lime juices, olive oil, salt, pepper, hot peppers and garlic in bowl. Add scallops and stir. Chill for at least 2 hours, stirring occasionally.

Combine the remaining ingredients, add to the scallop mixture, stirring gently, and allow to marinate for another hour.

Strain off some of the liquid, and serve scallops on lettuce leaves.

Serves 4.

— Frances McKenna
Ottawa, Ontario

SMOKED SALMON

⅓ cup salt
⅓ cup white sugar
⅓ cup brown sugar
1 Tbsp. pepper
1 Tbsp. lemon pepper

1 Tbsp. rosemary
1 Tbsp. dry barbecue spice
1 Tbsp. garlic powder
3-4 lbs. salmon fillets

Combine all ingredients except salmon and mix well. Cut fillets into pieces 4 to 5 inches long and ¾ inch thick. Sprinkle combined seasonings liberally on all sides of the fish. Let stand for 30 minutes, then place on racks of electric smoker, and smoke with hickory chips for 4 to 5 hours. Check every 30 minutes after the first 4 hours, and stop process when desired degree of dryness is reached.

Smoked fish will keep for 3 weeks in the refrigerator and several months in the freezer.

Makes 3 to 4 pounds.

— Donald Smillie
Calgary, Alberta

SALMON TARTARE

1⅓ lbs. salmon
2 egg yolks
1 Tbsp. olive oil
Juice of 1 lemon
1 Tbsp. Worcestershire sauce

1½ Tbsp. capers
1 Tbsp. minced onion
1½ tsp. mustard
Pepper

Mince salmon very finely. Whip egg yolks, then add olive oil drop by drop. Add lemon juice, Worcestershire sauce, capers, onion, mustard and pepper.

Toss salmon with sauce, chill well, then serve on buttered pumpernickel bread.

Serves 6.

— R. Hildred
Lasqueti Island, British Columbia

Soups & Stews

Here's a pretty kettle of fish!

– Iolanthe
William Schwenck Gilbert

CHINO'S SOUP

THIS RECIPE ORIGINATED IN A SMALL ROADSIDE STAND IN GUADALAJARA, MEXICO. THE SOUP makes a satisfying main course and, garnished with cold green avocado, has both taste and eye appeal.

1 Tbsp. olive oil
1 large onion, finely chopped
1 clove garlic, minced
19-oz. can plum tomatoes
2 carrots, cubed
3 stalks celery, chopped
4 bay leaves
7 cups fish stock
2 potatoes, cubed

1 lb. sea bass or red snapper fillets,
    cut into 1-inch pieces
½ lb. shrimp, peeled, deveined & cut
    into pieces
6 raw oysters
3 cups Salsa Cruda (recipe follows)
2 avocados, peeled & chopped
Lime wedges
Tabasco or other hot sauce

Heat oil in a large saucepan and sauté onion until tender. Add garlic, tomatoes, carrots, celery, bay leaves and fish stock. Simmer for 15 minutes. Add potatoes and cook until tender. Add fish and simmer for 5 minutes or until fish flakes. Just before serving, bring to a boil, add shrimp and oysters, then ladle immediately into deep bowls. Add a spoonful of cold Salsa Cruda and some avocado pieces. Serve with lime wedges and hot sauce.

Serves 6.

— Hazel Baker
Coombs, British Columbia

SALSA CRUDA

1 lb. fresh tomatoes
½ cup fresh coriander leaves (if unavailable, use
    parsley)
¾ cup finely chopped onion
1-4 fresh or canned hot peppers, finely
    chopped

Cut tomatoes into small cubes. Combine with remaining ingredients, stirring to blend.

Makes enough to accompany Chino's Soup, above.

— Hazel Baker
Coombs, British Columbia

ITALIAN FISH SOUP

1 lb. fish fillets
3 Tbsp. lemon juice
2-3 stalks celery, sliced
1 medium onion, thinly sliced
3-4 medium carrots, sliced
1½ Tbsp. butter
19-oz. can tomatoes

4 cups water
1 tsp. pepper
1½-2 tsp. oregano
½ tsp. basil
Bay, thyme, rosemary
1 tsp. garlic powder
¼-½ cup uncooked egg noodles

Cut fish into serving-sized pieces and sprinkle with lemon juice.

In a large pot, sauté celery, onion and carrots in butter, stirring until coated. Add tomatoes, water and spices and simmer for 20 minutes. Add noodles and simmer for another 10 to 15 minutes. Add fish and simmer for 20 minutes longer.

Serves 4.

— Marjorie Maund
Yellowknife, Northwest Territories

BERGEN FISH SOUP

Fish Stock
½ cup coarsely chopped turnip
½ cup coarsely chopped carrots
1 large yellow onion, coarsely chopped
1 potato, peeled & chopped
1 tsp. salt
6 whole black peppercorns
1 Tbsp. chopped parsley stems
1 bay leaf
3 stalks celery with leaves
2 lbs. fish trimmings (heads, bones, etc.), washed
4 quarts cold water

Soup
4 Tbsp. butter
4 Tbsp. flour
Fish stock
½ cup finely chopped carrots
¼ cup finely chopped parsnips
1 lb. boneless halibut, cod or haddock, in one piece
½ cup finely sliced leeks, white parts only
2 egg yolks
Salt & pepper
3 Tbsp. finely chopped parsley
6 Tbsp. sour cream

To prepare the fish stock, combine turnip, carrots, onion, potato, salt, peppercorns, parsley, bay leaf, celery and fish trimmings in a large, heavy saucepan. Add water and bring to boil. Cover the pan, lower heat and simmer for 30 to 40 minutes.

Strain the stock, discarding the vegetables and fish trimmings. Wash the saucepan and return the stock to it. Boil rapidly for 20 minutes to reduce stock to 6 cups. Strain again and set aside.

To make the soup, melt butter in large, heavy saucepan. Add flour and stir until mixed. Gradually add stock, stirring constantly as stock thickens. Add carrots, parsnips and fish. As soon as soup reaches a boil, lower heat and simmer, uncovered, for 10 minutes. Add leeks and simmer for 3 to 4 minutes longer. Remove from heat, lift out fish and set aside on a platter.

In a small bowl, beat egg yolks with wire whisk. Beat in ½ cup of hot soup, one tablespoon at a time. Pour this back into the soup in a thin stream, beating continuously with a whisk.

With a fork, separate fish into flakes and add to soup. Season with salt and pepper and reheat, but do not boil. To serve, garnish with parsley and sour cream.

Serves 6.

— Louise Ogloend
Hjelmeland, Norway

SALMON BISQUE

3 Tbsp. butter
1 onion, finely chopped
1 stalk celery, finely chopped
3 Tbsp. flour
3½ cups milk
7½-oz. can salmon
Salt & pepper

Melt butter in a saucepan and sauté onion and celery. Add flour and stir well. Add milk slowly, stirring constantly. Add salmon and season with salt and pepper. Cook over low heat until creamy and smooth. Cool, place in blender and blend until smooth. Reheat gently to serve.

Serves 4.

— Lynn Hill
Barry's Bay, Ontario

HUNGARIAN FISHERMAN'S BROTH

FISHERMAN'S BROTH WAS ORIGINALLY MADE ON THE BANKS OF THE DANUBE RIVER, USING THE crystal clear waters of that river. The men rose early and cast their lines from small rowboats or favourite banks. The women, arriving later, would set up a large cauldron, keeping the water boiling while they waited for their husbands to bring back the catch. Long strands of freshly made noodles hung drying from the low branches of river willows. Late in the morning, the fishermen came back with fish and stories, which were all put in the pot: carp, pike, bass, catfish, even the one that got away went in with the fresh onions, heaps of paprika and dried hot peppers. This soup has now become the traditional meal on Christmas Eve throughout the plains of Hungary.

2 potatoes, sliced
5 onions, thinly sliced
3-4 lbs. fish
Hot chili peppers

1 hot green pepper
2 Tbsp. paprika
Salt

Place potatoes in a deep pot. Place onions on top of the potatoes. Cut fish into large pieces and add them to the pot. Add enough water to cover fish, bring to a boil, then add remaining ingredients. Cook for 30 minutes over medium heat. The soup is strained and served over hot noodles. Add salt to taste.

Serves 6.

— Mary Andrasi
Acton Vale, Quebec

CACCIUCCO ALLA FLORENTINA

4 lbs. assorted fish (trout, bass, red snapper, etc.)
1 lobster
¾ cup olive oil
3 cloves garlic, minced
3 sprigs parsley
½ cup celery leaves
½ tsp. marjoram
1 Tbsp. salt
½ tsp. crushed chili peppers

2 cups dry red wine
1 cup dry white wine
2 cups water
¼ cup tomato paste
½ cup diced celery
2 cloves garlic, sliced
3 Tbsp. minced parsley
¼ tsp. thyme

Wash and dry fish and lobster. Remove heads, tails and bones from fish and reserve for stock. Cut up lobster, saving body for stock.

Heat ½ cup oil in large saucepan, then sauté minced garlic, parsley sprigs and celery leaves for 5 minutes. Add fish heads, bones, body of lobster, marjoram, salt, chili peppers, wines, water and tomato paste. Bring to a boil, then simmer over low heat for 45 minutes. Strain, pressing as much of the solids as possible into the stock.

Heat remaining oil in a large saucepan and sauté celery, sliced garlic, minced parsley and thyme for 5 minutes. Arrange fish on top of vegetables and pour the stock over the fish. Bring to a boil, cover and reduce heat to low. Simmer for 10 minutes. Add the lobster meat, cover and cook for 20 minutes. Adjust seasonings. Serve in deep bowls with toasted garlic bread.

Serves 8.

— Bruce Bodkin
Montreal, Quebec

FILE GUMBO

INTRODUCED TO THE CONTRIBUTOR BY HER FATHER-IN-LAW, THIS IS BETTER THE SECOND DAY and freezes well. Filé gumbo powder, a popular Creole seasoning, is ground sassafras leaves and is available in specialty food shops.

2 Tbsp. butter
1 large onion, sliced
1 clove garlic, sliced
2 Tbsp. flour
2 16-oz. cans tomatoes
1 lb. fresh okra or 2 10-oz. pkgs. frozen
2 tsp. Worcestershire sauce

¼ tsp. Tabasco sauce
7 cups water
6 Tbsp. oyster sauce
1 tsp. filé gumbo powder
1 lb. shrimp, shelled, deveined & cut into bite-sized pieces
1 lb. red snapper, filleted & cut into bite-sized pieces

Heat butter in a large saucepan, cook onions until tender, then add garlic and flour, stirring well. Add tomatoes and okra and cook until slightly thickened. Add Worcestershire sauce, Tabasco sauce, water and oyster sauce. Mix filé gumbo powder with a bit of the liquid to dissolve it and add to gumbo. Cook over low heat, covered, for 1 hour. Add shrimp and red snapper and simmer for 20 minutes.

Serves 6.

— Valeen Duncan
Carvel, Alberta

SHRIMP BISQUE

¼ cup butter
⅔ cup finely chopped mushrooms
1 carrot, finely chopped
1 onion, finely chopped
1 stalk celery, finely chopped
2 Tbsp. finely chopped parsley
1 bay leaf
½ tsp. peppercorns
1 tsp. sugar

¼ tsp. marjoram
¼ tsp. mace
1 Tbsp. lemon juice
2 cups chicken, turkey or fish stock
1½ cups small shrimp, cooked
½ cup sliced mushrooms
1 green onion, thinly sliced on the diagonal
½ cup whipping cream
Chopped green onion tops

Melt butter in large saucepan, add mushrooms, carrot, onion, celery, parsley, bay leaf, peppercorns, sugar, marjoram, mace and lemon juice. Simmer, covered, for 5 minutes, stirring once or twice. Add stock and simmer, covered, for 20 minutes. Press stock through a sieve, discard vegetables. Return broth to saucepan, add shrimp, mushroom slices and sliced green onion and heat through. Whip cream. Ladle soup into bowls and swirl some of the whipped cream into each serving. Garnish with green onion tops.

Serves 4.

— Judy Koster
Bridgewater, Nova Scotia

CAPE HOUSE INN ICED BUTTERMILK WITH SHRIMP SOUP

THE CONTRIBUTOR OF THIS RECIPE DISCOVERED THIS SOUP WHILE ON HOLIDAY IN NOVA SCOTIA. The owner of the Cape House Inn in Mahone Bay generously shared his recipe. This soup has come to be one of the all-time favourites of the *Harrowsmith* staff.

3 cups shrimp
3 quarts buttermilk
1½ English cucumbers, coarsely chopped
3 Tbsp. fresh dill weed
2 Tbsp. dry mustard

2 Tbsp. chopped dill pickle
1 Tbsp. salt
1 tsp. pepper
Cayenne

Cook shrimp in boiling water until tender. Peel and chop into 1-inch pieces. Combine all ingredients, adding cayenne to taste. Mix well and chill. Serve garnished with thin cucumber slices.

Serves 12.

— *Billie Sheffield*
North Gower, Ontario

CREAMY FISH & ALMOND SOUP

½ lb. fish fillets (cod, sole, haddock,
  Boston bluefish)
3 cups water
2 tsp. aniseed
1 large shallot, chopped

½ cup blanched almonds, ground
1 cup light cream
2 Tbsp. parsley, chopped
Salt
White pepper

Poach fish in water seasoned with aniseed and shallot until tender. Do not overcook. Strain, reserving liquid. Put fish and seasonings in blender and purée with almonds. Stir purée into reserved water, add cream and heat gently. Add parsley, and season to taste with salt and pepper.

Serves 6.

— *Katherine Dunster*
Golden, British Columbia

CREAM OF SALMON SOUP

1 small onion, minced
1 cup sliced mushrooms
4 Tbsp. butter
2 Tbsp. flour
½ tsp. salt

¾ tsp. dry mustard
¼ tsp. pepper
16-oz. can salmon
13-oz. can evaporated milk
1½ cups water

Cook onion and mushrooms in butter until onion is soft. Stir in flour, salt, mustard and pepper and cook for 1 minute. Add remaining ingredients and cook until heated through, but do not boil.

Serves 4.

— *Susan O'Neill*
Bella Coola, British Columbia

BASIC FISH CHOWDER

3 large potatoes, peeled & diced
2 lbs. haddock, cod or other white fish fillets
¼ lb. salt pork or bacon, diced
1 large onion, diced

1 Tbsp. ground ginger
6 cups milk
Salt & pepper
1 Tbsp. butter

Cook potatoes for 10 minutes in enough boiling water to cover. Add fish and cook a further 10 minutes or until fish flakes. Drain, reserving liquid. Flake fish, removing any bones. In a large saucepan, cook bacon or salt pork until crisp, add onion and ginger, and cook until onion becomes transparent. Add 2 cups of reserved liquid to the fish and potatoes. Add milk, heat through, then add bacon mixture and season with salt and pepper. Place butter to melt on soup just before serving.

Serves 8.

— *Mrs. Bruce L. Blakemore*
Cape Negro, Nova Scotia

EXTRAVAGANT FISH CHOWDER

½-¾ cup cooked lobster
½-¾ cup cooked shrimp
½-¾ cup cooked crabmeat
½-¾ cup fresh scallops, thinly sliced
½ lb. mushrooms, thinly sliced &
   sautéed in 4 Tbsp. butter

1 cup thick white sauce
½ cup milk
½ cup dry white wine
Salt & pepper
Parsley
Chives

Combine all ingredients except parsley and chives, and heat gently — do not boil. If using canned seafood, drain well before adding to the chowder. Season with salt and pepper. Garnish with parsley and chives.

Serves 4.

— *Joann Alho*
Brantford, Ontario

NEW ENGLAND CLAM CHOWDER

4 slices bacon, chopped
1 large onion, chopped
4 medium potatoes, diced
3 cups chicken stock
1 tsp. salt
½ tsp. pepper
2 Tbsp. butter

2 Tbsp. flour
3 cups light cream
2 10½-oz. cans baby clams, drained
1 cup clam juice
2 Tbsp. minced parsley
Paprika

Fry bacon in a large saucepan until crisp, then remove with a slotted spoon and reserve. Add onion to the saucepan, sauté until softened, then add potatoes and chicken stock. Season with salt and pepper, cover and cook for 15 minutes.

In a second saucepan, melt butter, then add flour, stirring to make a roux. Cook for 1 minute, then add light cream. Cook over low heat until thickened, then add to vegetables along with clams and clam juice, and heat through. Garnish each serving with parsley and paprika.

Serves 8 to 10.

— *Valerie Gillis*
Renfrew, Ontario

LOBSTER CHOWDER

6 potatoes, cubed
12 cups water
2 onions, chopped
3 Tbsp. butter
1 lb. lobster meat
Salt & pepper
1 cup milk

Cook potatoes in water. Fry onions in butter until tender, add lobster meat and cook, stirring, for a few minutes, then add to the cooked potatoes. Add salt and pepper to taste, then simmer, covered, for 15 minutes. Add milk and simmer for another 5 minutes.

Serves 6.

— Emilia Williams
Sable River, Nova Scotia

PACIFIC CHOWDER

1 cup butter
2 cups chopped onion
2 cups chicken stock
2 cups clam juice
2 cups chopped celery
6 medium carrots, coarsely chopped

2 lbs. halibut fillets
4 cups milk
⅔ cup flour
2 5-oz. cans clams, with juice
1 lb. small shrimp
Salt & pepper

Melt butter, add onions and cook until soft. Stir in chicken stock, clam juice, celery and carrots. Bring to a boil, lower heat and simmer until carrots are tender — 15 minutes.

Cut halibut fillets into chunks, add to the soup, cover and simmer for another 7 minutes.

Stir enough milk into the flour to make a paste, then stir this into the soup. Simmer for a few minutes, then add the remainder of the milk. Simmer, stirring, until it is thickened slightly. Do not let it boil or the milk will curdle. Add clams with their juice and shrimp. Heat through, stirring occasionally. Season with salt and pepper and serve.

Serves 8.

— Irene Louden
Port Coquitlam, British Columbia

DESOLATION SOUND OYSTER CHOWDER

THE CONTRIBUTOR IMPROVISED THIS RECIPE AFTER PRYING SOME HUGE OYSTERS OFF THE ROCKS while on a cruise to Desolation Sound in her boat. The basil and oregano really enhance the flavour of the oysters.

6-8 large oysters in their shells
4 slices bacon
⅓ cup flour
Salt & pepper
½ tsp. basil
½ tsp. oregano

1 onion, chopped
1 stalk celery, chopped
2 medium potatoes, diced
1 carrot, chopped
3 cups milk
2 Tbsp. butter

Shuck oysters and drain, reserving juice. Rinse, then place on paper towel to dry. Chop bacon and sauté. Combine flour with seasonings, dredge oysters in flour, then brown in bacon fat over medium heat. Remove oysters and bacon, and drain. Add remaining seasoned flour to bacon fat and stir for 1 minute. Add oyster juice and vegetables, with water if necessary. Simmer until vegetables are tender, stirring often. Chop oysters, add to vegetables, then add bacon. Stir in milk and butter. Heat gently, adjust seasonings and serve.

Serves 3 to 4.

— Wendy Vine
Ganges, British Columbia

Fillet of Sole Florentine, page 206

Chinese Shallow-Fried Noodles with Seafood, page 163

Pan Bagnat, page 130

Scallops with Baby Corn Cobs, page 165

Chino's Soup, page 106

Top to bottom, *Fish Kabobs, page 216; Marinated Barbecued Fish, page 217; Greek-Style Skewered Fish, page 217*

Top to bottom, *Bermuda Fish Chowder, page 121; Pacific Chowder, page 112; Cream of Salmon Soup, page 110*

Stuffed Lobster Tails, page 182

BERMUDA FISH CHOWDER

THE WARING HOUSE, LOCATED JUST OUTSIDE PICTON, ONTARIO, WAS FORMERLY A FAMILY residence and has been converted into an intimate, elegant restaurant. The chef's original approach to food is manifested in an unusual menu, from which this recipe is a selection.

19-oz. can tomatoes
½ lb. whitefish or perch fillets
½ tsp. fresh thyme
2 bay leaves
1 or 2 hot banana peppers, seeds removed

2 Tbsp. flour
2 Tbsp. butter
1 cup whipping cream
Salt & pepper
¼ cup dark rum

Cut tomatoes and fish into large chunks. Simmer with herbs and juice from can of tomatoes for 15 minutes. Add sliced banana peppers. In a small bowl, make a paste of the flour and butter, and stir into soup to thicken. Add cream and salt and pepper to taste, and heat gently. Ladle into bowls and pour 1 Tbsp. rum into each serving.

Serves 4.

— *Anita Vidal, The Waring House*
Picton, Ontario

MANHATTAN CLAM CHOWDER

2 slices bacon, diced
1 small onion, minced
2 stalks celery, finely chopped
7-oz. can baby clams
2 potatoes, diced

1 cup water
28-oz. can tomatoes
¼ tsp. thyme
Salt & pepper

Sauté bacon in saucepan with onion and celery until vegetables are tender but not brown. Drain clams, reserving juice. Add juice, potatoes and water to saucepan. Bring to a boil, reduce heat, and simmer for 15 minutes or until potatoes are tender. Add clams, tomatoes and seasonings. Heat through and serve.

Serves 6.

— *S. Hols*
Houston, British Columbia

PAT BAY CHOWDER

ALTHOUGH POLLUTION AND RED TIDES HAVE SPOILED THE CLAM GROUNDS FOR WHICH THIS recipe is named, there are still tidal areas on both coasts where anyone with a shovel and some patience can soon fill a pail with juicy clams. If you get your clams from the fishmonger, your meal will lack the adventure but not the taste.

1 lb. fresh clams
2 Tbsp. butter
1 large onion, chopped
1 clove garlic, minced
1 stalk celery, chopped
½ cup chopped mushrooms
2-3 ripe tomatoes, chopped
2 large potatoes, diced

1 large carrot, diced
7-oz. can tomato paste
¼ tsp. thyme
Salt & pepper
1 bay leaf
¼ cup dry white wine
3 cups water or vegetable stock
2 Tbsp. chopped parsley

Steam, shell and drain clams. Cut into bite-sized pieces.

Melt butter in a large saucepan, sauté onion, garlic, celery and mushrooms. Add all remaining ingredients except clams and parsley, and simmer for 30 minutes or until vegetables are tender. Add clams and parsley, heat and serve.

Serves 4.

— *Heather Quiney*
Victoria, British Columbia

MACKEREL CHOWDER

3 Tbsp. butter
2 Tbsp. finely chopped onion
2 cups corn
2 Tbsp. flour
28-oz. can tomatoes
2 cups water
1 Tbsp. sugar
1 tsp. salt

¼ tsp. pepper
Tabasco sauce
Worcestershire sauce
½ tsp. basil
1 cup green beans
7-oz. can mackerel, drained & flaked
1 cup milk, scalded

Heat butter in medium saucepan. Add onion, sauté for 1 minute, stirring, then add corn and cook, stirring, for another 3 minutes. Sprinkle in flour, stir to blend in, then remove from heat. Add remaining ingredients except for beans, mackerel and milk.

Bring to a boil, stirring. Reduce heat, cover and simmer for 20 minutes. Add green beans and simmer for another 10 minutes, stirring occasionally. Add mackerel and milk and simmer for 5 more minutes.

Serves 4 to 6.

— Shelley Townsend
Lethbridge, Alberta

CURRIED CHOWDER

1 lb. ocean perch fillets
2 medium onions, chopped
2 Tbsp. butter
1 Tbsp. curry powder
1 tsp. paprika

1 tsp. chili powder
1 tsp. sugar
2 cloves garlic, crushed
28-oz. can tomatoes
Salt & pepper

Cut perch into 1½-inch pieces. Sauté onions in butter, sprinkle with seasonings, then add garlic and tomatoes. Bring to a boil and stir in fish. Simmer, covered, for 15 to 20 minutes, stirring occasionally to break up tomatoes.

Serves 4.

— Irene Louden
Port Coquitlam, British Columbia

QUICK FISH CHOWDER

THIS CHOWDER HAS BETTER FLAVOUR IF REHEATED THE DAY AFTER IT IS MADE.

1 onion, chopped
1 stalk celery, chopped
1 small green pepper, chopped
¼ cup butter
19-oz. can tomatoes
2 cups water
1 cup long grain white rice
2-3 cups vegetable or tomato juice

2 Tbsp. pickling spice
2 cloves garlic, quartered
1 lb. fish fillets, cut into 1-inch pieces
1 tsp. paprika
1 tsp. Worcestershire sauce
2-3 drops Tabasco sauce
Salt & pepper

Sauté onion, celery and green pepper in butter until soft. Add tomatoes, water, rice and juice. Tie pickling spice and garlic in a piece of cheesecloth, and add to soup. Simmer until rice is tender — 20 to 30 minutes. Add fish and seasonings. Simmer for 10 minutes or until fish flakes easily. Remove cheesecloth.

Serves 6.

— Wendy Vine
Ganges, British Columbia

FISHERMAN'S LUCK SOUP

USE THE CATCH OF THE DAY IN THIS HEARTY SOUP.

½ cup oil
3 medium onions, chopped
2 potatoes, chopped
2 carrots, chopped
2 cloves garlic, chopped
2 lbs. fish, cleaned, boned & cut into chunks
4 ripe tomatoes or 1 cup canned tomatoes
1 bay leaf

1 Tbsp. chopped fennel
1 sprig thyme
2 Tbsp. chopped parsley
2-3 cups water or fish stock
1 can clams with juice
1 tsp. lemon juice
Salt & pepper
6 slices crusty bread

Heat oil in a large saucepan. Sauté onions, potatoes, carrots and garlic until just browned, stirring to prevent sticking. Add fish, tomatoes, bay leaf, fennel, thyme, parsley and stock or water. Cover and simmer for 15 to 20 minutes. Add clams with juice. Simmer for 6 to 8 minutes. Add lemon juice and adjust seasonings.

Heat slices of bread in oven at 250 degrees F until crisp and dry. Place a slice of bread in each bowl, and ladle hot soup over bread and serve.

Serves 6.

— Irene Louden
Port Coquitlam, British Columbia

SHRIMP CREOLE SOUP

1 onion, chopped
2 stalks celery, sliced
Butter
26-oz. can whole tomatoes, with juice
1 zucchini, sliced
2 carrots, sliced
1 tsp. curry

½ tsp. oregano
½ tsp. thyme
½ tsp. salt
Pepper
¾ cup raw rice
3 cups water
1-1½ lbs. shrimp, shelled & deveined

Sauté onion and celery in butter until just tender. Add remaining vegetables and seasonings and bring to a boil. Add rice and water, cover and reduce heat. Simmer for 20 to 30 minutes. Uncover, add shrimp and cook for another 3 minutes. Do not overcook the shrimp.

Serves 6.

— M. Kasparek
Nepean, Ontario

FISH STEW

THIS RECIPE WON TOP PRIZE IN A CONTEST SPONSORED BY THE *Sarnia Observer* IN 1982. OTHER vegetables, such as peas, beans, summer squash or corn, may also be used.

2 Tbsp. butter
1 large onion, chopped
1 clove garlic, crushed
2 leeks, chopped
1 stalk celery, chopped
1 green pepper, finely chopped
1 cup canned or chopped fresh tomatoes

Salt, pepper, thyme & basil
1½ cups fish stock, water or white wine
1 potato, cubed
2 carrots, sliced
1 lb. fish fillets, cut into 1-inch cubes
Parsley, chopped

In a large saucepan, melt butter, add onion, garlic, leeks, celery and green pepper and cook until softened. Add tomatoes, seasonings and liquid. Add potato and carrots, cover and simmer until vegetables are tender. Add fish, cover and simmer for 5 to 10 minutes or until fish flakes. Adjust seasonings and garnish with parsley.

Serves 4.

— Nan Millette
Corunna, Ontario

CIOPPINO

INDIGENOUS TO THE GULF COAST OF THE UNITED STATES, THIS SEAFOOD GUMBO RECALLS THE influence of Italians who fished the coast 100 years ago. Somewhat elaborate to prepare, it makes a delightful supper when served with fresh greens and crusty bread.

½ cup olive oil
4 onions, chopped
1 green pepper, chopped
4 cloves garlic, minced
28-oz. can tomatoes
7-oz. can tomato paste
2 cups red wine
1 lemon, thinly sliced
1 Tbsp. basil

1 tsp. oregano
1 cup chopped parsley
1½ lbs. ocean perch, cut into
    1½-inch pieces
2 small lobsters, cut up
1 lb. shrimp, shelled & deveined
24 mussels, cleaned
Salt & pepper

Heat oil in large saucepan. Sauté onions, green pepper and garlic until tender. Add tomatoes, tomato paste, wine, lemon slices, basil, oregano and half the parsley. Bring to a boil, reduce heat and simmer for 20 minutes. Add perch and lobster, cover and simmer for 10 minutes. Add shrimp and simmer a further 10 minutes. Add mussels and simmer, covered, for 5 minutes or until mussels open. Season with salt and pepper. Ladle into bowls and garnish with remaining parsley.

Serves 8.

BAKALAW

THIS IS A FILIPINO CODFISH STEW.

1 lb. salt cod, rinsed, & soaked
    overnight in cold water
1 clove garlic, crushed
2 Tbsp. oil
2 onions, chopped

2 potatoes, diced
28-oz. can tomatoes
2 tsp. chopped parsley
½ cup water
2 cups peas

Drain cod and cut into 1-inch pieces. In heavy saucepan, brown garlic in oil. Remove from heat, discard garlic and add fish, stirring to brown. Add remaining ingredients, cover and simmer for 30 minutes. (If frozen peas are used rather than fresh, add during last 10 minutes of cooking.)

Serves 6.

— Helen Shepherd
Lansdowne, Ontario

GHANIAN FISH STEW

1 lb. fish fillets (perch, Boston
    bluefish, haddock), cut into 1-inch
    chunks
1 egg, beaten
Flour
1 tsp. salt
¼ tsp. pepper
¼ tsp. cayenne

¼ cup oil
2 large onions, sliced
1 large green pepper, chopped
2 banana peppers, seeded & sliced
    into rings
3 tomatoes, peeled & mashed
1 Tbsp. tomato paste
28-oz. can tomatoes

Dip fish in egg, then dredge with flour that has been seasoned with salt, pepper and cayenne. Set aside.

In 1 Tbsp. oil, sauté onions, green pepper and banana peppers until tender. Stir in fresh tomatoes. Simmer for 5 minutes, then place in a larger saucepan. Heat remaining oil, and brown fish quickly on all sides. Add to vegetables along with tomato paste and canned tomatoes. Simmer for 10 minutes before serving.

Serves 4.

— Judit E. G. Smits
Saskatoon, Saskatchewan

BOUILLABAISSE

A RICH FISH STOCK AND THE FINEST SELECTION OF SEAFOOD AVAILABLE ARE NECESSARY TO transform a stew into an event.

½ cup olive oil
4 large onions, thinly sliced
2 stalks celery, chopped
4 cloves garlic, minced
8 tomatoes, peeled & chopped
Bouquet garni (thyme, bay leaf,
   parsley, peel of 1 orange)
½ cup chopped fresh fennel
7-oz. can tomato paste
2 cups dry white wine
1 tsp. saffron threads
6 cups rich fish stock

2 lbs. lobster, boiled for 10 minutes,
   shelled & cut into pieces
1 lb. halibut, cut into 2-inch chunks
1 lb. turbot, cut into 2-inch chunks
1 lb. pickerel, cut into 2-inch chunks
½ lb. shrimp, peeled & deveined
Salt & pepper

Loaf of crusty bread, sliced
2 Tbsp. olive oil
½ cup grated Parmesan cheese
1 cup Sauce Rouille (recipe follows)

Heat ½ cup oil in a large, heavy-bottomed pot. Sauté onions, celery and garlic until tender. Add tomatoes, bouquet garni, fennel, tomato paste, wine and saffron. Cook for 10 minutes, then add 5 cups stock. Simmer for 30 minutes. Remove bouquet garni.

Add lobster, halibut and turbot. Cover and simmer for 5 minutes. Add pickerel and shrimp and simmer for 5 minutes or until shrimp is pink and fish flakes. Season with salt and pepper.

Brush slices of bread with remaining 2 Tbsp. oil and sprinkle with cheese. Brown lightly in oven. Place a slice of bread in each bowl, spoon chunks of fish onto bread, then ladle broth over fish. Pass Sauce Rouille in a separate bowl.

Serves 8 to 10.

SAUCE ROUILLE

1 jar pimentos
4 cloves garlic, minced
¼ cup olive oil
½ cup fresh bread crumbs
1 cup hot fish stock (reserved from
   Bouillabaisse recipe)

Combine pimentos, garlic, olive oil and bread crumbs in a blender. Blend until smooth. Add hot stock and blend. Serve with Bouillabaisse.

FISH STOCK

FISH TRIMMINGS CAN BE ACCUMULATED IN THE FREEZER UNTIL YOU HAVE ENOUGH FOR A BATCH of stock. Avoid strong-tasting, oily fish.

2 lbs. fish heads, tails, bones & trimmings
1 onion, halved
1 cup mushroom pieces
Parsley
Thyme

1 bay leaf
1 Tbsp. lemon juice
4 cups water
1 cup dry white wine

Bring all ingredients to a boil. Reduce heat, skim foam off surface and simmer for 30 minutes. Strain carefully before using or freezing.

Makes approximately 4 cups stock.

ESSENCE OF SHELLFISH

1 lb. shells from crab, shrimp, lobster
Parsley
4 green onions
1 bay leaf
6 peppercorns
2 cups water
2 cups dry white wine

Bring all ingredients to a boil. Reduce heat, skim surface, and simmer for 30 minutes. Strain.

Makes approximately 3 cups.

SHELLFISH STEAMING JUICE

3 cups white wine
1 onion, finely chopped
3 cloves garlic, finely chopped
1 cup chopped parsley
¼-½ cup butter
6 lbs. mussels or clams

Combine all ingredients except mussels or clams in large stock pot with lid. Heat almost to the boiling , add shellfish, then heat until shells open.

Serves 6 to 8.

— *Pieter Timmermans*
Ucluelet, British Columbia

COURT BOUILLON

COURT BOUILLON CAN BE USED AS A SOUP BASE OR AS A MEDIUM FOR POACHING FISH. IT HAS A delicate flavour and aroma, which enhances the natural flavour of the fish that it is poaching.

1½ cups white wine
6½ cups water
2 carrots, quartered
5 shallots, chopped
2 leeks, chopped
2 sprigs tarragon
2 sprigs thyme
1 bay leaf
6 sprigs parsley
12 peppercorns
Juice of 3 lemons

Combine all ingredients except lemon juice in large, heavy stock pot. Bring to a boil, reduce heat to low, cover and simmer for 20 minutes. Strain. Add lemon juice.

The Court Bouillon can be refrigerated for a few days or frozen until it is needed.

Makes approximately 10 cups.

Salads
& Sandwiches

Owing to the fact that fish . . . is easily digestible,
it is an excellent food for sedentary workers.

– Larousse Gastronomique

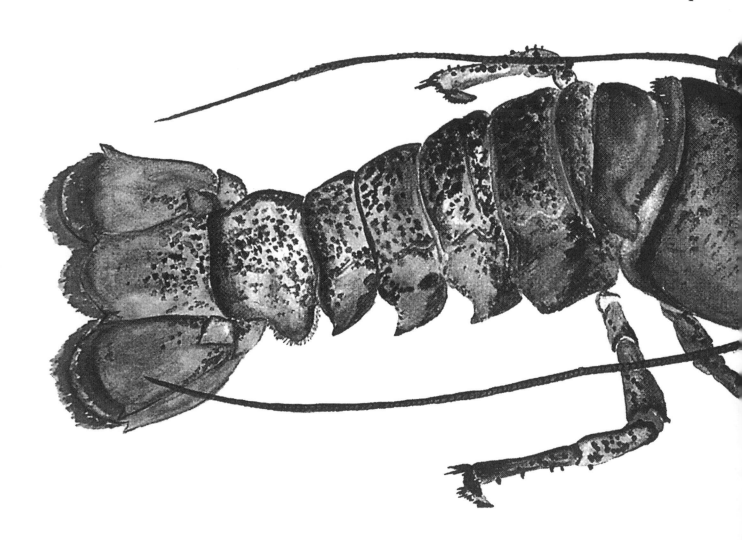

PAN BAGNAT

THIS DISH IS A PROVENCALE SANDWICH WITH A NORTH AFRICAN INFLUENCE. THE HARISSA sauce should be made a day ahead, then the actual assembly of the sandwich takes very little time.

Harissa Sauce
1 Tbsp. olive oil
2-3 small hot chili peppers
1½ Tbsp. wine vinegar

Sandwich
4 round crusty buns or sections of baguette
   cut on bias
1 can anchovies

6½-oz. can tuna
2 tomatoes, sliced
1 onion, sliced
1 green pepper, cut into thin strips
4 leaves romaine lettuce, torn in half
16 small black olives, split & pitted
3 Tbsp. olive oil
Pepper

To make harissa sauce, gently heat olive oil and finely diced chili peppers. Remove from heat, add vinegar and allow to marinate for at least 12 hours.

Slice buns or bread and generously sprinkle olive oil on bottom halves. On each sandwich, place 2 anchovies, 1 Tbsp. tuna, 3 slices tomato, 2 slices onion, ½ lettuce leaf and several strips of green pepper. Sprinkle with olives, pepper and remaining olive oil. Cover with top half of bun, pressing gently.

Serve with harissa sauce.

Serves 4.

— *Gwenda Wells*
Alcove, Quebec

HOT CRABMEAT SANDWICHES

½ cup slivered almonds
6½-oz. can crabmeat
¼ cup chopped celery
¼ cup mayonnaise
1 Tbsp. lemon juice

1 ripe avocado, peeled & chopped
3 English muffins,
   split, toasted & buttered
1 cup grated Cheddar cheese
Tomato wedges

Place almonds on baking sheet and bake at 350 degrees F for 3 to 5 minutes.

Drain crabmeat. Combine celery, almonds, mayonnaise, lemon juice and avocado with crabmeat and toss lightly.

Arrange toasted muffin halves on baking sheet, cover with crab mixture and top with cheese. Bake at 400 degrees F for 15 minutes or until topping is heated through and cheese is melted. Serve with tomato wedges.

Serves 6.

— *Judi Knopfl*
Coquitlam, British Columbia

B.C. BURGER

1 slice smoked salmon
2 slices whole wheat bread
Mayonnaise
6 smoked oysters
2 ½-inch slices cream cheese

Sliced tomato
Lettuce
Thin slice red onion
Sprouts

Barbecue or broil salmon until heated. Place on bread with mayonnaise and top with oysters, cheese, tomato, lettuce, onion and sprouts.

Serves 1.

— *Gillian Barber-Gifford*
Rossland, British Columbia

ANTIPASTO MELT

1 cup tomato sauce
2 cups thinly sliced mushrooms
2 Tbsp. minced onion
1 cup thinly sliced black or
    green olives
¼ cup vegetable oil

½ lb. old Cheddar cheese, grated
1 clove garlic, minced
1 cup seafood
    (tuna, salmon, cooked shrimp)
¼ cup finely chopped sweet pickles
4 kaiser buns, split in half

Combine all ingredients except buns. Spread on each half of bun and broil at 450 degrees F for 5 to 6 minutes or until bubbly.

Serves 4.

— Pat Dicer
Mission, British Columbia

HEAVENLY LUNCH

6½-oz. can crabmeat
11-oz. can oysters
6½-oz. can shrimp
½ cup mayonnaise
1 Tbsp. Dijon mustard

1 avocado, chopped
4-6 croissants
4 oz. cream cheese
½ cucumber, sliced
Alfalfa sprouts

Combine crabmeat, oysters, shrimp, mayonnaise and mustard. Make a pocket in each croissant and spread with cream cheese. Stuff with seafood mixture and top with cucumbers, avocado and a handful of sprouts.

Serves 4 to 6.

— Gillian Barber-Gifford
Rossland, British Columbia

SPICED TUNA POCKETS

1 cup cooked flaked tuna
¼ cup mayonnaise
½ tsp. curry powder
¼ tsp. chili powder
1 tomato, chopped
1 small avocado, finely chopped

1 Tbsp. chopped parsley
2 pieces pita bread
Bean sprouts
¼ cup toasted flaked almonds

Combine tuna, mayonnaise, curry powder, chili powder, tomato, avocado and parsley.

Wrap pita breads in foil and heat at 250 degrees F for 10 minutes. Divide tuna mixture between breads and top with sprouts and almonds.

Serves 2.

— Judi Knopfl
Coquitlam, British Columbia

TUNA SUBMARINE

1 loaf French bread, about 15 inches long
2 7½-oz. cans tuna, drained & flaked
½ cup mayonnaise

½ cup chopped dill pickle
½ cup chopped celery
1 cup grated Cheddar cheese

Cut top from bread, lengthwise. Hollow out bottom, leaving a ¾-inch shell. Tear half the remaining bread into small pieces and combine with other ingredients. Spoon mixture into bottom portion of bread, then cover with top. Wrap in foil, then bake at 400 degrees F for 30 minutes.

Serves 6.

— Nan Millette
Corunna, Ontario

BRITISH COLUMBIA BENEDICT

1 English muffin
Butter
2 eggs

2 generous slices smoked salmon
2 slices Swiss cheese
¼ cup Hollandaise sauce

Split muffin. Toast both halves, then lightly butter them. Meanwhile, poach eggs. Place salmon on muffin and top with cheese, egg and Hollandaise sauce. Broil for 2 minutes.

Serves 1.

— Gillian Barber-Gifford
Rossland, British Columbia

CURRIED SHRIMP, GRAPE & CASHEW SALAD

A DELICIOUS SAVORY-SWEET SALAD WITH GREAT TEXTURAL VARIETY, THIS MAKES AN IDEAL picnic lunch on a hot summer day.

1 lb. cooked, cleaned shrimp
2 cups seedless green grapes
1½ cups roasted, salted cashews
½ cup sour cream
½ cup mayonnaise
2 Tbsp. minced onion

2 Tbsp. finely chopped green pepper
1 Tbsp. lemon juice
1½-2½ tsp. curry powder
½ tsp. freshly grated ginger
Bunches of green grapes to garnish

Cut shrimp in half, or, if very large, into bite-sized pieces. Combine with grapes and cashews in salad bowl. Combine remaining ingredients except grapes and serve with salad and grapes. Dressing will develop in flavour if prepared the night before and refrigerated.

Serves 4 to 6.

— Ron Myhr
Claremont, Ontario

AVOCADO & SHRIMP VINAIGRETTE

1 large avocado
½ lb. shrimp
½ cup oil
3 Tbsp. vinegar
½ tsp. salt
¼ tsp. pepper

1 clove garlic, crushed
1 tsp. finely chopped onion
2 Tbsp. finely chopped
   dill pickle
1 egg, hard boiled
   & finely chopped

Cut avocado in half, peel and remove pit. Fill with shrimp. Combine remaining ingredients in jar and shake well. Pour over shrimp.

Serves 2.

— Colette McFarland
Telkwa, British Columbia

AIOLI SALAD PLATTER

AIOLI IS NOTHING MORE THAN A GARLIC MAYONNAISE, QUICKLY ASSEMBLED AND VERY
delicious. It can be served with whatever fresh vegetables and seafood are available.

½ lb. fresh green beans
1 lb. cooked large shrimp
1 egg
1½ Tbsp. white wine vinegar
1½ Tbsp. lemon juice
1 tsp. salt

1 tsp. Dijon mustard
4 cloves garlic, peeled
½ cup oil
½ cup olive oil
2 cups cherry tomatoes
¾ lb. mushrooms

Cook green beans and drain well. Shell and devein shrimp. Refrigerate beans and shrimp.
Place egg, vinegar, lemon juice, salt, mustard and garlic in blender. Blend for a few
seconds. With motor running, gradually add oils in a slow steady stream until a thick
mayonnaise results. Refrigerate.

At serving time, arrange tomatoes, mushrooms, beans and shrimp on a large platter.
Mound sauce in a serving bowl and pass with salad platter.

Serves 8 as an appetizer.

— Sylvia Petz
Willowdale, Ontario

SHRIMP TOMATO ASPIC

2 envelopes gelatin
½ cup cold water
2½ cups tomato juice
½ tsp. salt
⅛ tsp. cloves
3 bay leaves
1 tsp. sugar

2 Tbsp. vinegar
1 tsp. horseradish
1 cup diced celery
¼ cup diced green pepper
¼ cup sliced stuffed olives
1 cup cooked shrimp

Sprinkle gelatin over cold water and set aside.

Combine tomato juice, salt, cloves, bay leaves, sugar and vinegar. Place in saucepan and
bring to a boil. Remove from heat, add gelatin and stir to dissolve. Remove bay leaves.

Chill until quite thick, then add horseradish, celery, green pepper, olives and shrimp. Pour
into mould. Chill until firm, then unmould on bed of lettuce or spinach.

Serves 6 to 8.

— Frieda Meding
Trochu, Alberta

SHRIMP STUFFED TOMATOES

A LIGHT AND ATTRACTIVE LUNCHEON DISH, THIS RECIPE CAN BE ALTERED TO USE CHERRY
tomatoes instead, in which case it would make delicious finger fare for a buffet meal.

4 large tomatoes
1½ cups chopped cooked shrimp
2 green onions, finely chopped
2 Tbsp. butter, softened
1 tsp. chopped parsley

1 small clove garlic, crushed
4 oz. cream cheese, softened
1 tsp. Dijon mustard
1 Tbsp. lemon juice
Salt & pepper

Slice off tops of tomatoes and scoop out the pulp. Set upside down on paper towels to
drain for 10 minutes. Combine remaining ingredients, seasoning to taste. Stuff tomatoes
with mixture and refrigerate until well chilled.

Serves 4.

— Jane Meszaros
Sturgeon Falls, Ontario

ORANGE AND SHRIMP SALAD

4 oranges
1 cup cooked shrimp
4 green onions, cut
  into bite-sized pieces
½ cup diced celery
¼ cup chopped fresh parsley
½ cup diced cucumber

Salt & pepper
2 Tbsp. olive oil
1 Tbsp. lemon juice
¼ cup mayonnaise
½ tsp. dry mustard
1 tsp. honey
1 clove garlic, crushed

Peel oranges and cut into bite-sized pieces. Place in bowl and add shrimp, green onions, celery, parsley, cucumber and salt and pepper.

Combine remaining ingredients to make dressing. Mix well and pour over salad, tossing lightly.

Serves 4.

— Joanne Lavallee
St. Côme, Quebec

MARINATED MUSSELS

48 mussels in the shell
2 cloves garlic, thinly sliced
1 Tbsp. dried tarragon
1 tsp. salt

1 tsp. pepper
¼ cup chopped sweet onion
⅔ cup olive oil
⅓ cup light vinegar or lemon juice

Scrub mussels in cold water, discarding any which do not close when put in water. Pull off beards with fingers. Place one inch of water in bottom of large saucepan and bring to a boil. Add mussels, cover, and reduce heat to medium and cook for 3 to 5 minutes. Mussels are cooked when shells open.

Drain, and discard any mussels that have not opened. Combine remaining ingredients in bowl. When mussels are cool enough to handle, remove from shells, add to marinade, cover and refrigerate overnight.

Serve on a bed of lettuce.

Serves 8.

MARY'S SEAFOOD MUSHROOM MASTERPIECE

Dressing
3 hard-boiled egg yolks
2 Tbsp. Dijon mustard
2 Tbsp. herb or wine vinegar
⅔ cup safflower oil

Salad
½ lb. cooked shrimp or salmon
½ lb. mushrooms, sliced

¼ lb. feta cheese, crumbled
10 radishes, sliced
1 red onion, thinly sliced
½ English cucumber, thinly sliced
Lettuce or spinach leaves for garnish

Combine egg yolks, mustard and vinegar in blender. Blend until smooth, then add oil in a steady stream to make a creamy dressing.

Combine remaining ingredients except lettuce or spinach leaves and toss with dressing. Serve on bed of lettuce or spinach leaves.

Serves 4 to 6.

— Mary Bailey
Lethbridge, Alberta

SCANDINAVIAN HOT CAULIFLOWER WITH SHRIMP SAUCE

THIS MAKES A SPECTACULAR PRESENTATION FOR A BUFFET BUT IS EQUALLY DELICIOUS WHEN THE sauce is served over chopped, steamed cauliflower.

1 large cauliflower
Boiling water to cover

Sauce
2 cups milk
1 onion, thinly sliced
2 sprigs dill or parsley
¼ cup butter
¼ cup flour

1 tsp. salt
¼ tsp. white pepper
2 cups cooked shrimp, chopped or
  whole
¼ cup whipping cream
Fresh dill or parsley to garnish

Trim, wash and cook whole cauliflower until it is barely tender, about 30 minutes.

Combine milk, onion and dill or parsley and bring to a boil. Strain into a bowl. In same saucepan, melt butter, stir in flour and cook over low heat for 2 minutes. Stir in hot milk. Cook, stirring constantly, until mixture is thick and smooth. Season with salt and pepper. Add shrimp, then heat through gently. Whip cream and fold into sauce. Place cauliflower on a serving platter, then pour sauce over. Garnish with dill or parsley and serve immediately.

Serves 6 to 8.

— *Holly Andrews*
Puslinch, Ontario

FISHERMAN'S TREAT

2 cups water
2 Tbsp. lemon juice
½ tsp. salt
1 bay leaf
1 tsp. minced onion
1 lb. scallops
4-5 potatoes, cut in half
1 cup sliced green beans
1 cup olive oil

⅓ cup tarragon vinegar
Salt & pepper
1 cup mayonnaise
½ cup sour cream
¼ cup chopped parsley
½ tsp. dill weed
1 Tbsp. horseradish
1 cup thinly sliced celery

Combine water, lemon juice, salt, bay leaf and minced onion in saucepan and bring to a boil. Add scallops, reduce heat, cover and simmer for 5 minutes. Drain, then cut scallops in half.

Cook potatoes in water until tender, then cool and slice ¼-inch thick. Cook beans until just tender.

Combine oil, vinegar, salt and pepper and marinate scallops, potatoes and beans in this for at least 2 hours, refrigerated.

Combine remaining ingredients and mix with scallops, potatoes and beans, toss gently and serve.

Serves 8.

— *Colleen Beckley*
Terrace, British Columbia

OCTOPUS SALAD

OCTOPUS IS QUITE READILY AVAILABLE IN SUPERMARKETS IN CANADA, SO, ALTHOUGH THIS recipe originated on the shores of the Mediterranean, it can be duplicated successfully here.

1 lb. octopus
⅓ cup olive oil
Juice of 1 lemon

¼ cup chopped parsley
2-3 cloves garlic, crushed
Chopped hot pepper to taste

Remove ink sac from octopus, then boil octopus until tender. Cut into bite-sized pieces and season with olive oil, lemon juice, parsley, garlic and pepper. Chill and serve.

Serves 6 as an appetizer.

— Hazel Baker
Coombs, British Columbia

SEAFOOD LETTUCE ROLLS

½ cup chopped lobster meat
½ cup crabmeat
½ cup flaked, cooked salmon
½ cup cooked shrimp
2 Tbsp. chopped parsley
½ cup sour cream

⅓ cup mayonnaise
½ tsp. dry mustard
¼ tsp. salt
⅛ tsp. pepper
¼ cup diced celery
Romaine lettuce

Combine all ingredients except lettuce in a bowl. Place a few spoonfuls of the mixture on each lettuce leaf, roll leaf over mixture and secure with a toothpick.

Serves 4 to 6.

— Joanne Lavallee
St. Côme, Quebec

SEABREEZE SALAD

2 cups cooked crabmeat
2 tart apples, cored & diced
2 hard-boiled eggs, chopped
2 cups cooked, diced potatoes
2 Tbsp. minced onion
½ cup chopped celery

½ cup chopped green pepper
1 cup seedless raisins,
   scalded (optional)
1 cup mayonnaise
½ cup whipping cream, whipped
1 tsp. lemon juice

Combine crabmeat, apples, eggs, potatoes, onion, celery, green pepper and raisins. Whisk together mayonnaise, whipping cream and lemon juice. Pour dressing over salad. Mix gently to combine and chill well before serving.

Serves 6.

— Mary Giesz
Winfield, British Columbia

BEAN AND TUNA SALAD

6½-oz. can tuna
1½ cups cooked lima beans
Olive oil
Vinegar
1 Tbsp. chopped green onions

1 Tbsp. chopped parsley
1 clove garlic, crushed
Salt & pepper
2 eggs, hard boiled
Mayonnaise

Drain tuna and mix together with beans in a large bowl. Add oil and vinegar to taste. Mix in green onions, parsley, garlic and salt and pepper. Slice eggs and arrange on top of salad. Serve accompanied by mayonnaise.

Serves 6.

— Iris Bates
Midhurst, Ontario

CRAB LOUIS

2 tsp. chili sauce
2 tsp. chopped green onion
1 tsp. vinegar
1 tsp. horseradish
1 tsp. mustard
½ tsp. sugar
¼ tsp. paprika
Salt & pepper

½ cup mayonnaise
½ cup sour cream
1 lb. crabmeat,
    cooked & cut into chunks
1 head lettuce
2-3 hard-boiled eggs, sliced
1 cucumber, sliced

Combine chili sauce, green onion, vinegar, horseradish, mustard, sugar, paprika, salt, pepper, mayonnaise and sour cream. Toss with crabmeat.

Shred lettuce and line serving bowl with it. Top with crabmeat mixture and surround with egg and cucumber slices.

Serves 6.

— J. Bertrand
High Level, Alberta

RHINELAND HERRING SALAD

6 pickled herring fillets, chopped
3 medium beets, cooked & diced
1 large apple, diced
2 medium potatoes, cooked & diced
1 small onion, finely chopped
½ cup chopped walnuts

½ cup sour cream
½ cup mayonnaise
1 tsp. sugar
1 egg, hard cooked & sliced
6-8 slices beet
1 Tbsp. chopped parsley or dill

Combine all ingredients except egg, sliced beet and parsley or dill and mix gently together. Arrange in salad bowl or on serving platter. Garnish with egg and beet slices and sprinkle with parsley or dill.

Serves 4 to 6.

— Sylvia Petz
Willowdale, Ontario

DILLED FISH SALAD

2 lbs. sole or halibut
1 stalk celery, broken in half
1 slice lemon
5 peppercorns
Salt

1½ lbs. cooked shrimp
2 tsp. lemon juice
2 Tbsp. dill weed
¾ cup mayonnaise

Cover fish with water and poach for 8 minutes with celery, lemon slice, peppercorns and salt. Remove fish from water and break into bite-sized pieces.

Rinse shrimp under cold water and add to fish.

Mix together lemon juice, dill weed and mayonnaise. Combine with fish and shrimp, tossing lightly.

Serves 8.

— Denyse Fournier
Ottawa, Ontario

DILLED SHRIMP & CAPPELLINI SALAD

½ cup dry white wine
⅓ cup white wine vinegar
1½ cups olive oil
3 Tbsp. finely chopped dill weed
2 tsp. salt

Pepper
1½ lbs. shrimp, shelled, cooked
    & sliced lengthwise in half
1½ lbs. cappellini, cooked,
    drained & rinsed

Combine wine, vinegar, oil, dill, salt and pepper, and mix well. Add shrimp, and let marinate for at least 30 minutes. Pour over cappellini, toss to coat well, and serve.

Serves 6.

PASTA SALAD NICOISE

⅓ cup oil
3 Tbsp. lemon juice
3 Tbsp. vinegar
½ tsp. salt
½ tsp. dry mustard
½ tsp. paprika
½ tsp. basil
8 oz. linguine

1 cup sliced green beans, cooked,
   drained & chilled
1 cup halved cherry tomatoes
¼ cup sliced, pitted ripe olives
12½-oz. can tuna, chilled & drained
3 hard-cooked eggs, sliced

To make dressing, combine oil, lemon juice, vinegar, salt, mustard, paprika and basil in a screw-top jar. Cover, and shake well to mix.

Cook linguine, drain, and rinse under cold water. Pour dressing over linguine, and toss gently to coat. Cover, and chill for several hours.

Combine chilled linguine, green beans, cherry tomatoes and olives in salad bowl, tossing to mix. Break tuna into bite-sized chunks, and mound on top of salad. Garnish with sliced eggs.

Serves 6.

— Christine Taylor
Norbertville, Quebec

SEAFOOD SALAD

A SIMPLE AND COOL LUNCHEON DISH FOR HOT SUNNY DAYS.

1½ cups chopped celery
2 Tbsp. finely chopped onion
½ cup chopped green pepper

2 cups cooked small macaroni shells
1 7½-oz. can tuna, drained
¾ cup mayonnaise

Combine all ingredients, mixing gently but thoroughly. Chill well.

Serves 4.

— Lynn Hill
Barry's Bay, Ontario

FISH DUMPLINGS (FISKEFARCE)

1 lb. fish fillets, skinned & boned
   (sole, pickerel, cod)
2 tsp. salt
¼ tsp. white pepper
5 Tbsp. flour

2 Tbsp. butter, softened
2 eggs
2½-3½ cups light cream
4 cups water or fish stock

Grind fish fillets 2 to 3 times, then mix with salt, pepper and flour. Stir vigorously and work in butter. Add eggs, one at a time, stirring well. Gradually add enough cream to make a rather stiff mixture that can be dropped from a spoon.

Bring 4 cups salted water or stock to a boil, then cook one spoonful of the mixture to check for consistency. If mixture is too stiff, add more cream. If it is too soft, beat in an extra egg. Cook the dumplings a few at a time for 6 to 8 minutes, keeping cooked ones warm in the oven until they are served. Serve well drained with shrimp or asparagus sauce.

Serves 4 to 6.

— Alexis Mathison-Smith
White Rock, British Columbia

PICKLED HERRING

6 herring
¼ cup salt
2½ cups water
2½ cups malt vinegar

1 Tbsp. mixed pickling spice
1 dried chili pepper
1 bay leaf
1 large onion, finely sliced

Clean and bone herring. Dissolve salt in water and pour over herring.

While herring is in brine, bring vinegar and pickling spice slowly to a boil. Remove from heat and let sit for 30 minutes, then strain and cool. Pour over herring, then add chili pepper, bay leaf and sliced onion.

Cover and leave in a cool place for 5 to 6 days before using. The herring can be stored for several months.

Makes 1 quart.

— Rosalind Hildred
Lasqueti Island, British Columbia

MARINATED SQUID

1 lb. squid, cleaned
1 cup red wine vinegar
½ lemon, thinly sliced
1 bay leaf

Marinade
½ cup oil

¼ cup red wine vinegar
2 cloves garlic, minced
1 tsp. minced parsley
1-2 tsp. minced oregano
¼ tsp. salt
Pepper

Cut squid body sacs in quarters lengthwise. Cut tentacles in half. Bring 1 cup vinegar to a boil with 1 cup water, lemon slices and bay leaf. Add squid and cook for 30 seconds to 1 minute. Transfer squid to strainer, drain well, then rinse with cold running water.

Meanwhile, assemble marinade ingredients. Add squid and let stand, stirring occasionally, for at least two hours.

Chill well.

Serves 4.

— Frances McKenna
Ottawa, Ontario

MURRAY'S MARINATED OCTOPUS

THE CONTRIBUTOR FIRST TASTED THIS RECIPE WHEN HE WAS WORKING FOR THE BRITISH Columbia Forest Service. His boat was anchored alongside a prawn boat, and the fishermen gave him some octopus that had inadvertently become caught in the prawn traps. The workcrew cook prepared this recipe.

2 lbs. octopus
2 bottles beer

Marinade
¼ cup vinegar

¼ cup soya sauce
¼ cup white wine
2 Tbsp. finely chopped onion

Clean and skin octopus, then pound tentacles. Heat beer to boiling point and simmer octopus in it for 10 minutes. Chop into bite-sized pieces.

Combine marinade ingredients and mix well. Add octopus and marinate refrigerated overnight.

Serves 6 to 8.

— Garry Beaudry
Hagensburg, British Columbia

Quiches & Pies

Ruling a big country is like
cooking a small fish.

– The Way of Lao-tzu
Lao-tzu

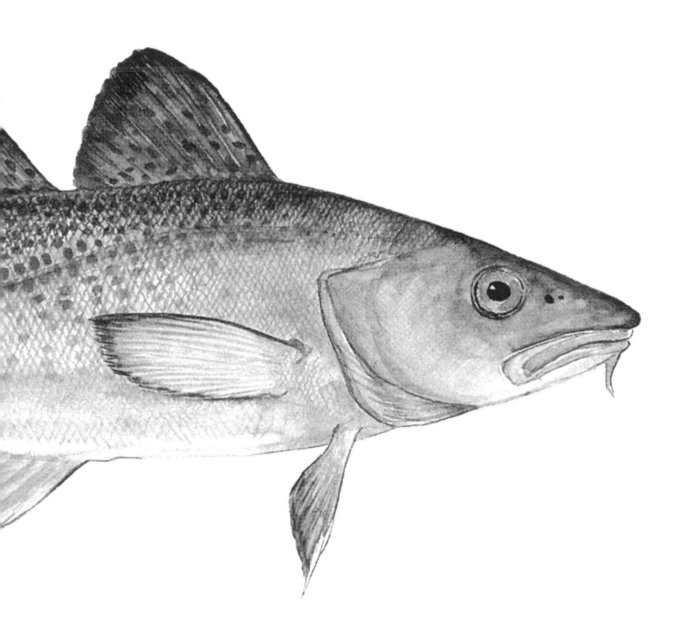

CRAB CAMEMBERT QUICHE

Pastry for 10-inch pie
1 cup crabmeat
½ lb. Camembert cheese
4 green onions, chopped

4 eggs
1 cup heavy cream
2 Tbsp. sour cream
Salt & pepper

Sprinkle crabmeat over pastry shell, then top with sliced Camembert cheese and green onions.

Beat eggs, cream and sour cream together. Season with salt and pepper, then pour over cheese and crabmeat. Bake at 425 degrees F for 10 minutes, reduce temperature to 350 degrees F and bake for another 15 to 20 minutes or until filling is set.

Serves 4.

— Wendy Dodd
Frobisher Bay, Northwest Territories

ANNE'S SPECIAL QUICHE

1 pie shell
½ cup sour cream or yogurt
2 eggs
2 Tbsp. prepared mustard
½ lb. cream cheese, softened
2 blocks tofu
2 tsp. whole wheat flour

2 7¾-oz. cans salmon, drained & flaked
½ lb. broccoli
¼ lb. mushrooms, sliced & lightly
   sautéed
¼ cup grated Swiss cheese
12 chopped, pitted black olives

Bake pie shell at 375 degrees F for 10 minutes, then remove from oven and set aside.

Combine sour cream or yogurt, eggs, mustard, cream cheese, tofu and flour in blender and process until smooth.

Arrange salmon in bottom of pie shell and top with chopped broccoli.

Pour cream cheese mixture over broccoli and cover with mushrooms. Sprinkle with cheese and cover with olives.

Bake at 375 degrees F for 40 to 45 minutes or until knife comes out clean.

Serves 6.

— Anne Henderson
Stoney Creek, Ontario

SALMON QUICHE

Crust

1½ cups whole wheat pastry flour
½ cup grated Cheddar cheese
⅓ cup finely chopped almonds
½ tsp. salt
¼ tsp. paprika
½ cup oil

3 eggs
1 cup sour cream
¼ cup mayonnaise
2 Tbsp. finely chopped green onion
½ tsp. dried dill
½ cup cubed Cheddar cheese

Filling

16-oz. tin salmon

Combine all crust ingredients except oil. Stir in oil and press into 9-inch pie plate. Bake for 10 minutes at 400 degrees F.

Drain fish, reserving liquid. Add eggs, sour cream, mayonnaise, onion and dill to the salmon liquid. Stir in fish and cheese, mixing well. Pour into crust, then bake at 375 degrees F for 45 minutes or until centre is firm.

Serves 6.

— Pat Dicer
Mission, British Columbia

B.C. QUICHE

Crust for 10-inch pie
8 oz. cream cheese, thinly sliced
2½-3 cups chopped smoked or fresh salmon
1 small can green chilies, chopped
1 cup sliced mushrooms
½ cup chopped scallions

4 Tbsp. butter
4 eggs
1 cup light cream
Fresh dill, parsley & basil
Salt & pepper
Paprika

Bake pie crust at 400 degrees F for 10 minutes, then cool. Line cooled shell with cream cheese and top with salmon and chilies.

Meanwhile, sauté mushrooms and scallions in butter, then place on top of the salmon. Whisk together eggs and cream. Add seasonings. Pour over pie and sprinkle with paprika.

Bake at 425 degrees F for 10 minutes, reduce heat to 350 degrees and cook for another 30 minutes or until custard is firm. Let stand for 15 minutes before serving.

Serves 6.

— Gillian Barber-Gifford
Rossland, British Columbia

CRUSTLESS QUICHE WITH SHRIMP

¼ cup butter, melted
10 eggs, beaten
½ cup flour
1 tsp. baking powder
1 tsp. salt

1 cup diced green & red pepper
2 cups cottage cheese
1 lb. Swiss cheese, grated
1 cup minced onion
1 lb. shrimp, cooked & shelled

Combine butter, eggs, flour, baking powder and salt. Mix well. Stir in remaining ingredients, combining thoroughly.

Pour into lightly greased 9" x 13" baking pan. Bake at 400 degrees F for 15 minutes, then reduce heat to 350 degrees F and bake for another 45 minutes or until knife inserted into centre comes out clean.

Serves 8 to 12.

— Mary Bailey
Lethbridge, Alberta

KOKANEE NUT PIE

1½ cups whole wheat flour
½ tsp. salt
½ tsp. paprika
½ cup butter
1½ cups grated Cheddar cheese
⅓ cup chopped nuts
1 lb. salmon, cooked & flaked

3 eggs, beaten
1 cup sour cream
¼ cup mayonnaise
1 Tbsp. minced onion
3 drops Tabasco sauce
1 tsp. dill weed

Combine flour, salt and paprika, then cut in butter and 1 cup cheese until mixture resembles coarse meal. Stir in nuts.

Set aside 1 cup of this mixture and press remainder into bottom and up sides of 10-inch pie plate. Combine remaining ingredients and place in pie plate. Top with remaining crumb mixture and rest of cheese.

Bake at 350 degrees F for 35 minutes.

Serves 6.

— Linda Vineyard
Seattle, Washington

COULIBIAC

3 Tbsp. butter
1 onion, finely chopped
½ cup rice
1 cup chicken stock
4 Tbsp. dill weed
4 hard-boiled eggs, cut into eighths
1 lb. mushrooms, sliced, sautéed
   & sprinkled with lemon juice

Salt & pepper
1 tsp. nutmeg
½ cup white wine
4-lb. salmon, poached & cooled
1½ pkgs. puff pastry
1 egg, beaten

Melt butter and sauté onion for 5 minutes. Add rice and cook, stirring, for another minute. Add chicken stock, reduce heat, cover and simmer for 15 minutes, or until rice is soft.

Place rice in large mixing bowl and add dill weed, eggs, mushrooms, salt and pepper, nutmeg and wine. Mix well.

Remove skin and backbone from salmon.

Roll out half the pastry until it measures 18″ x 9″. Place salmon on pastry and heap dressing mixture up around it. Roll out remaining dough to a slightly larger rectangle and drape it around the fish. Press pastry edges together to seal. Brush with beaten egg and make a hole in top for steam to escape.

Bake at 400 degrees F for 1 hour.

Serves 8 to 10.

— Judy Koster
Bridgewater, Nova Scotia

SALMON WELLINGTON

4-5-lb. salmon

Dressing
¼ cup cooked rice
3-4 green onions, chopped
½ cup chopped shrimp
½ cup sliced mushrooms
2 Tbsp. lemon juice

2 tsp. sage
Salt & pepper

Pastry
3 cups flour
1 tsp. baking powder
Salt
1 cup shortening

Clean and scale salmon, but leave head, tail and fins on.

Combine dressing ingredients and stuff cavity of salmon.

Combine flour, baking powder and salt, and cut in shortening until mixture resembles small peas. Work in enough water to make a rollable dough.

Roll pastry out large enough to completely enclose salmon. Place salmon on pastry, wrap with dough, then cut dough away from face and tail. Wrap tail in foil so it won't burn during cooking. Bake at 350 degrees F until pastry is brown and salmon is cooked — 45 to 60 minutes.

Serves 8.

— Isabelle Hewitt
Courtenay, British Columbia

YEAST PASTRY

¼ cup unsalted butter
2½ cups flour
1 tsp. salt

½ Tbsp. yeast
3 Tbsp. lukewarm water
3 eggs, beaten

Cut butter into flour and add salt. Dissolve yeast in water, then add eggs.

Make a well in flour-butter mixture, and pour in yeast and eggs. Knead into flour until dough is smooth and no longer sticky, adding more flour, if necessary.

Shape into ball, place in buttered bowl, cover loosely and let rise for 1 hour. Punch down and roll out.

LOBSTER PIE

Pastry for single-crust pie
3 Tbsp. butter
3 Tbsp. finely chopped green onion
1½ cups cooked lobster
1 Tbsp. tomato paste

Cayenne pepper
4 eggs
1½ cups light cream
¼ cup grated Gruyère cheese

Prebake pie shell for 15 minutes at 375 degrees F. Cool. Melt butter, add onion and sauté for 2 minutes. Add lobster and cook over low heat, stirring, for 2 minutes. Add tomato paste and cayenne pepper. Cook, stirring, until mixture comes to a boil. Remove from heat and cool.

Beat eggs, add cream and stir into lobster mixture. Pour into crust, sprinkle with cheese and bake at 325 degrees F for 25 to 30 minutes.

Serves 6 to 8.

— *Irene Louden*
Port Coquitlam, British Columbia

MADAGASCAR SUNFISH

Pastry for double-crust pie
2 lbs. turbot fillets
8-oz. can tuna
½ cup finely chopped celery

¼ cup finely chopped onion
½ tsp. basil
½ tsp. celery salt

Roll pastry out into 2 oval shapes. Place 1 oval on cookie sheet. Arrange half the turbot fillets on pastry.

Combine tuna, celery, onion, basil and celery salt, and mound in the centre of the fillets. Place remaining fillets on top of tuna mixture, followed by the second oval pastry crust.

Trim pastry into shape of a fish, and use the trimmings to form fins, mouth and eyes. Seal the layers around the edge with water, and use the back of a spoon to make scales.

Bake at 350 degrees F for 45 minutes.

Serves 4 to 6.

— *Renate Seiler*
Carleton Place, Ontario

SEA URCHIN CREPES

THIS RECIPE COMES FROM SOINTULA, IN THE QUEEN CHARLOTTE STRAIT. THE ROE FROM SEA urchins is very popular there, and this recipe is a favourite. Served with a light Hollandaise sauce, it makes a delicious luncheon dish. It is important to remember to wear protective gloves if gathering the urchins yourself. Use strong clippers or kitchen shears to cut out the underside limpet and free the roe. To make 2 cups of roe, you will need about 15 urchins.

2 cups roe
¼ cup melted butter
1¼ cups flour
½ tsp. salt

1 tsp. baking powder
1 cup milk
Dill pickles, finely chopped

Combine roe, melted butter and salt. Stir in half the milk. Sift flour and baking powder together, add to batter and stir briefly. Add remaining milk and beat briskly. Refrigerate for 2 hours.

Pour a small amount of batter onto a moderately hot, greased skillet. Tilt pan to spread batter thinly and evenly. Brown on both sides, then remove from skillet. Repeat until all batter is used up. Place a teaspoonful or two of finely chopped dill pickle on each crêpe, and roll. Top with Hollandaise sauce and serve.

Makes 16 to 20 crepes.

— *Cameron Norman*
South Gillies, Ontario

CRAB PASTRY CUPS

1¼ cups flour
1 tsp. salt
½ cup lard
Water
½ cup butter

2½-3 Tbsp. flour
2 cups light cream
3 oz. lobster pâté
6 oz. crabmeat
Salt & pepper

Combine flour and salt and cut in lard until mixture resembles small peas. Add water gradually to make a workable dough. Roll out and cut into circles to fit 12 muffin tins. Place in tins, stab each with a fork and bake at 400 degrees F until golden brown — approximately 10 to 15 minutes.

Meanwhile, prepare filling. Melt butter in double boiler. Add flour and mix well. Gradually stir in cream and cook, stirring, until mixture thickens. Add pâté, crabmeat and salt and pepper to taste. Stir well.

Fill pastry cups with crab mixture and serve immediately.

Makes 12 tarts.

— B. MacNeil
Pictou, Nova Scotia

SALMON IN PASTRY

2 medium onions, chopped
1 clove garlic, minced
2 Tbsp. butter
½ cup fresh bread crumbs
⅓ cup Parmesan cheese
Pastry for 9-inch double-crust pie

3 hard-boiled eggs
½ lb. salmon, cooked & flaked
⅓ cup finely chopped fresh dill
1 cup sour cream
1 egg
¼ tsp. salt

Sauté onions and garlic in butter until tender but not brown. Combine bread crumbs and cheese. Roll out half the pastry to an 8" x 10" rectangle ⅛" thick. Place on a baking sheet. Sprinkle with half the crumb mixture, half the onion mixture, the sliced hard-boiled eggs, the salmon and the dill. Sprinkle remaining onion mixture and remaining crumb mixture over salmon. Spread with sour cream. Mix egg and salt, then brush edges of pastry. Roll out remaining pastry and fit over top of filling, pressing edges with a fork to seal. Brush with egg mixture, then make three or four slits in the pastry to allow steam to escape. Bake at 375 degrees F for 45 minutes to 1 hour or until golden brown. Let rest for 10 minutes before serving.

Serves 4.

— Nancy Blenkinsop
Corbyville, Ontario

SALMON STUFFED POTATOES

2 large potatoes
1 Tbsp. sour cream
2 Tbsp. grated Parmesan cheese

1 Tbsp. chopped chives
7½-oz. tin red salmon

Bake potatoes at 350 degrees F until tender — about 1 to 1½ hours. Cut a thin slice off one side and scoop out pulp leaving skins intact.

Mash potatoes coarsely. Add sour cream, cheese and chives and mix thoroughly.

Flake salmon and add, along with the juice, to the potato mixture. Spoon this into the potato skins until heaping full. Sprinkle with additional Parmesan cheese to taste and reheat at 400 degrees F for 10 minutes.

Serves 2.

— Goldie Connell
Prescott, Ontario

SEAFOOD PUFF PIE

1¼ cups light cream
1 shallot, chopped
1 tsp. fresh thyme
1 tsp. fresh dill
1 bay leaf
Salt & pepper
¼ cup butter

¼ cup flour
½ lb. cod fillets, cooked & flaked
½ lb. shrimp, cooked
½ cup chopped parsley
1 tsp. lemon juice
12-oz. package puff pastry
1 egg yolk, beaten

Simmer cream, shallot, thyme, dill, bay leaf and salt and pepper in a saucepan over low heat for 10 minutes. Strain into a bowl, discarding seasonings. Melt butter in a saucepan, stir in flour and cook over low heat for 1 minute. Add cream, stirring constantly until sauce is thick and smooth. Remove from heat and add cod, shrimp, parsley and lemon juice. Set aside to cool.

On a lightly floured board, roll out puff pastry to ¼-inch thickness. Moisten edges with cold water, then place on baking sheet. Spoon mixture onto centre of pastry. Lift each corner of pastry and fold to centre, pinching carefully to seal. Brush with beaten egg yolk, then bake at 375 degrees F for 30 to 40 minutes or until golden brown.

Serves 4.

— Katherine Dunster
Golden, British Columbia

TUNA FISH PIE

Filling
⅓ cup butter
½ cup celery, chopped
¼ cup onion, chopped
3 Tbsp. flour
½ tsp. salt
3 cups milk
2 7½-oz. cans tuna, drained

Cheese Biscuit
1½ cups flour
1 Tbsp. baking powder
½ tsp. salt
3 Tbsp. butter
½ cup milk
¾ cup grated Cheddar cheese

To prepare the filling, melt butter, then add celery and onion and cook until softened, then stir in flour and salt. Blend in milk, stirring until thickened, then add tuna. Turn mixture into baking dish.

Sift flour, baking powder and salt together. Cut in butter, then stir in milk to make a soft dough. Knead for 2 minutes, then roll out on a lightly floured board to make an 8" x 10" rectangle. Sprinkle with cheese, then roll up, starting from the narrow end. Cut into 8 slices and place on top of tuna mixture. Bake at 450 degrees F for about 30 minutes.

Serves 4.

— Lynn Hill
Barry's Bay, Ontario

Stovetops

I have other fish to fry.

— **Don Quixote**
Cervantes

SOLE AMANDINE

THIS IS A VERY DELICATE AND BEAUTIFUL DISH. FOR ITS TRUE FLAVOUR, BE SURE TO GET Dover sole. Unless specified as Dover sole, most sole in North America refers to flounder, a similar flat fish.

1½ lbs. Dover sole fillets
½ cup flour
¼ cup plus 2 Tbsp. butter
½ cup dry white wine
5 thin slices lemon

Juice of 1 lemon
½ cup blanched, sliced almonds
Salt & pepper
1 Tbsp. chopped parsley

Dredge fillets in flour, and sauté in ¼ cup butter for 2 minutes on each side. Add wine, lemon slices and lemon juice and simmer for 3 minutes.

In a second pan, melt remaining 2 Tbsp. butter, add almonds and sauté until light brown.

Place fillets on a serving platter. Sprinkle with salt and pepper to taste. Pour sauce from pan over fish. Sprinkle with almonds and parsley and serve immediately.

Serves 4

— Lynn Hill
Barry's Bay, Ontario

FILLETS OF SOLE WITH LEEKS & SHRIMP

2 cups sliced leeks, white part only
½ cup butter
8 oz. shrimp, cooked, shelled & chopped
2 Tbsp. chopped dill weed
1 cup whipping cream

⅔ cup dry white wine
Salt & white pepper
Lemon juice
4 sole fillets
Flour

Cook leeks in ¼ cup butter over medium heat for 5 minutes. Stir in shrimp and dill and cook for 1 minute. Add cream, wine, salt and pepper and lemon juice to taste, and simmer for 10 minutes, or until thickened. Set aside and keep warm.

Dust sole with flour and sauté in remaining ¼ cup butter over medium-high heat until golden and flaky. Transfer to heated platter and pour sauce over.

Serves 4.

— Pam Collacott
North Gower, Ontario

FISH DUGLERE

1½ lbs. sole fillets
Salt & pepper
4 Tbsp. butter
1 onion, minced
1 stalk celery, minced
1 clove garlic, minced
1 cup well-drained canned tomatoes

¼ cup minced parsley
¼ cup white wine
5 thin slices lemon
¼ cup light cream
1 Tbsp. butter, softened
1 Tbsp. flour

Sprinkle fish with salt and pepper. Melt butter in heavy skillet, then add onion, celery and garlic. Sauté for 3 to 5 minutes. Top with fish, tomatoes, 1 Tbsp. parsley and wine. Place lemon slices over this.

Cut a circle of wax paper to fit skillet and place over mixture. Bring to a boil, cover with lid and cook over high heat for 5 to 10 minutes — until fish flakes easily but is still moist. Remove cover and paper. Pour cream around fish.

Mix 1 Tbsp. butter and flour. Add a little of the hot cream, mix, then stir into cream in skillet. Cook until sauce thickens. Sprinkle with remaining parsley.

Serves 6.

— Mara Smelters Wier
Toronto, Ontario

FILLETS CAPRICE

1 tsp. salt
¼ cup flour
2 Tbsp. milk
1 egg, beaten
1 lb. sole fillets
½ cup fine dry bread crumbs

Oil
1 large banana
2 tsp. lemon juice
3 Tbsp. melted butter
2 Tbsp. blanched slivered almonds

Combine salt with flour, and milk with egg in 2 shallow bowls. Dip fillets in flour, then in egg and then in bread crumbs.

Heat ¼ inch oil in heavy skillet until hot but not smoking. Pan-fry fillets until cooked through and golden brown. Remove to heated platter and keep warm.

Peel banana and cut in half lengthwise and then crosswise. Sprinkle with lemon juice and coat with remaining bread crumbs. Pan-fry in 2 Tbsp. butter until golden brown. Place on platter with fish. Toast almonds in remaining tablespoon of butter until brown, stirring often. Sprinkle over fish and bananas.

Serves 4.

— *Iris Bates*
Midhurst, Ontario

SEAFOOD BAHAI

THIS RECIPE WAS GIVEN TO THE CONTRIBUTOR BY A BRAZILIAN FRIEND. EASY TO MAKE, IT IS a delicious initiation to eating fish for those who think they do not like it.

2 Tbsp. butter
2 large onions, finely chopped
3 large cloves garlic, crushed
6-8 tomatoes, peeled
Salt & pepper

½ tsp. Tabasco sauce
1 cup concentrated coconut milk (bring 2 cups water to boil, add 1 cup grated coconut, simmer for ½ hour, then strain)
2 lbs. sole or flounder fillets

Melt butter and sauté onions and garlic. Mash tomatoes and add to skillet. Bring to a boil and let simmer for 15 to 20 minutes, then add salt and pepper and Tabasco sauce. Remove from heat, stir in coconut milk and return to heat. Add fillets and cook until heated through — 10 to 15 minutes.

Serves 4 to 6.

— *Inge Benda*
Bridgetown, Nova Scotia

FLOUNDER FRANCESE

1 lb. flounder or sole fillets
Flour
1 egg
1 Tbsp. milk

⅓ cup butter
3 Tbsp. oil
Juice from ½ lemon
Lemon wedges

Dust fillets with flour. Mix together egg and milk. Melt butter and oil in a skillet over medium heat and add lemon juice.

When oil-butter mixture begins to foam, dip fillets in egg and milk mixture. Place in skillet and fry for 2 to 3 minutes on each side. Serve immediately with lemon wedges.

Serves 4.

— *Nancy Doyle*
Secaucus, New Jersey

SPRING SALMON WITH CREAM & CHIVE SAUCE

1 large head romaine lettuce
2-3 stalks celery
1-2 carrots
1 leek
2 Tbsp. butter
3 cups fish stock
1 cup white wine

Salt & white pepper
1 onion, chopped
Juice of ½ lemon
4 slices fresh salmon fillets
1 bunch chives
2 cups light cream
¼ cup butter

Dip lettuce leaves in boiling water and rinse in cold water.

Cut celery, carrots and leek in julienne style. Blanch for 2 minutes in boiling water, then sauté in 2 Tbsp. butter for 3 or 4 minutes. Combine stock, wine, salt and pepper, onion and lemon juice.

Spread out lettuce leaves, grouping 3 or 4 together to form one serving. Salt and pepper salmon and place on lettuce leaves. Spread vegetables on top and fold as for cabbage rolls. Simmer in fish stock for 10 to 15 minutes.

Remove rolls from stock and keep warm. Reduce stock to one-third, add chives and cream and heat until slightly thickened. Whisk in butter and pour sauce around salmon. Garnish with parsley.

Serves 4.

— Ascona Place Restaurant
Gravenhurst, Ontario

SALMON WITH CHAMPAGNE SAUCE

4 salmon steaks
4 Tbsp. lemon juice

Stock
1 onion
2 carrots
¼ cup chopped parsley
½ tsp. dill weed
¼ tsp. tarragon
5 peppercorns
3½ cups water
1 cup white wine
Salt

Topping
1 avocado
6 oz. shrimp
4 Tbsp. mayonnaise
1 Tbsp. catsup
¼ tsp. white pepper

Sauce
3 egg yolks
1 tsp. cornstarch
⅔ cup champagne
Salt & white pepper
½ tsp. dried lemon balm

Marinate fish in lemon juice while preparing stock.

For stock, cut onion in half and carrots into quarters. Combine with parsley, dill, tarragon, peppercorns and water. Bring to a boil, reduce heat and simmer for 20 minutes, then add wine and salt.

Steam salmon over stock for 15 to 20 minutes, or until salmon flakes easily.

For topping, cube avocado, then combine with remaining ingredients.

To make sauce, combine egg yolks, cornstarch, champagne, salt and pepper in double boiler. Cook, stirring, over boiling water for 10 minutes or until sauce begins to thicken. Add lemon balm.

Place salmon on serving plate, top with shrimp and avocado mixture and serve with sauce.

Serves 4.

— Trudi Keillor
Berwyn, Alberta

HOT CREOLE SALMON

WHEN WE TESTED THIS RECIPE IN THE *Harrowsmith* KITCHEN, WE TRIED IT WITH TUNA AS WELL, which resulted in an equally delicious taste.

4 jalapeño peppers, minced
½ cup minced onions
2 stalks celery, minced
⅓ cup butter
⅓ cup flour
⅛ tsp. cayenne
⅛ tsp. white pepper

1 clove garlic, minced
½ tsp. paprika
2 cups fish stock
1 cup sliced, sautéed mushrooms
16 oz. cooked flaked salmon
½ cup grated Emmenthal cheese

Sauté peppers, onions and celery in butter until transparent. Add flour and spices and cook, stirring constantly, for 4 to 5 minutes. Add stock and cook for another 5 minutes over medium heat. Add mushrooms, salmon and cheese and cook over low heat until cheese is melted and mixture is heated through.

Serves 4.

— *Martin Foss*
Ashton, Ontario

SALMON POACHED IN VEGETABLES

1 Spanish onion, sliced
1 green pepper, cut in strips
½ lb. whole mushrooms
6 ripe tomatoes, chopped
3 cloves garlic, minced
1 tsp. salt
Pepper

4 salmon steaks
½ cup red wine
¼ cup coarsely chopped dill weed
Lemon juice
Lemon slices
Dill weed

Sauté onion, green pepper and mushrooms in large pan for 10 minutes. Add tomatoes, garlic, salt and pepper and simmer for 5 minutes. Arrange salmon on top of vegetables and pour wine over salmon. Place dill on top, cover and simmer for 10 minutes for every inch of fish. Remove cover and continue to cook for another 5 minutes to allow some of the liquid to evaporate.

Sprinkle with lemon juice and garnish with lemon slices and fresh dill.

Serves 4.

— *Lisa Calzonetti*
Elora, Ontario

SALMON SUKIYAKI

ORIGINALLY GIVEN TO THE CONTRIBUTOR BY A JAPANESE FISHERMAN ON THE WEST COAST OF Vancouver Island, this dish is good hot, served on rice, or cold.

3 lbs. fresh salmon
1-inch piece fresh ginger, peeled & thinly sliced
2-3 cloves garlic, crushed
¼ cup brown sugar
½ cup soya sauce
¼ cup mirin (rice wine), dry vermouth, white
   wine or sherry

Remove bones from salmon, cut fillets into 1-inch-wide strips. In a wok or skillet, combine remaining ingredients and heat to simmering. Add salmon and fry until done – about 5 minutes. If pan is too small to accommodate all the fish at once, fry in batches, removing cooked pieces with a slotted spoon and keeping warm until cooking is complete.

Serves 6.

— *Greg James*
Courtenay, British Columbia

POACHED RED SNAPPER WITH LOBSTER SAUCE

1½ cups white wine
Leafy end of 1 stalk celery
2 slices onion
¼-½ tsp. thyme
3 black peppercorns
¼ tsp. basil
2 sprigs parsley

4 fillets red snapper
¼ cup butter
3 Tbsp. flour
½ cup light cream
⅛ tsp. turmeric
½ lb. lobster meat, cut into chunks
3 Tbsp. grated Parmesan cheese

Combine wine with celery, onion, thyme, peppercorns, basil and parsley in saucepan. Bring to a boil, reduce heat and add fish. Poach gently, uncovered, for 7 to 10 minutes — until fish is just cooked. Remove fish from pan, cover, and keep warm in oven. Strain poaching liquid and reserve.

Melt butter in saucepan and stir in flour. Cook, stirring, for about 30 seconds. Add cream a little at a time, stirring constantly, then add enough poaching liquid to make a medium-thick sauce. Stir in turmeric. Cook gently, stirring, for 1 minute. Add lobster and cook until heated through, remove from heat and stir in Parmesan cheese.

Pour sauce over snapper and serve.

Serves 4.

— *Jane van der Est*
Vancouver, British Columbia

RED SNAPPER WITH TOMATOES

2 lbs. red snapper fillets
4 tomatoes, peeled,
   seeded & chopped
2 Tbsp. butter
1 small onion, chopped
1 cup white wine

1 Tbsp. chopped parsley
¼ cup cream
Juice of ½ lemon
1 Tbsp. cornstarch dissolved in 2 Tbsp.
   wine or cold water

Place fish in skillet and top with tomatoes. Add butter, onion and wine. Cover tightly and simmer for 10 minutes. Transfer fish to hot serving dish and keep warm.

Reduce fish cooking liquid to ½ cup. Add parsley, cream and lemon juice, then stir in cornstarch to thicken sauce. Pour over fish and serve.

Serves 4.

— *Valerie Marien*
Orangeville, Ontario

SHARK STEAKS WITH FRUIT SAUCE

IF YOU ARE UNABLE TO FIND SHARK STEAKS, TURBOT OR OTHER WHITE FISH CAN BE SUBSTITUTED successfully.

2 lbs. shark steaks
2 Tbsp. lemon juice
1 tsp. salt
1 Tbsp. cornstarch
1 Tbsp. sugar
¼ cup orange juice
¼ cup grapefruit juice

½ cup water
2 tsp. grated orange rind
1 tsp. lemon juice
2 mandarin oranges, broken
   into segments
1 cup green grapes, halved & seeded

Place shark steaks in well-greased skillet. Add 2 cups boiling water, lemon juice and salt. Cover and simmer for 8 to 10 minutes.

Meanwhile, prepare sauce. Combine cornstarch and sugar in small pot. Stir in orange and grapefruit juices and ½ cup cold water. Cook slowly, stirring constantly, until thickened. Stir in orange rind, lemon juice and fruit and heat thoroughly. Spoon sauce over fish and serve.

Serves 6.

— *Christine Taylor*
Norbertville, Quebec

KEDGEREE OF SALMON

1 Tbsp. butter
1 Tbsp. flour
½ tsp. curry powder
1 cup hot milk

7½-oz. can salmon
2 hard-boiled eggs
Salt & pepper

Melt butter and stir in flour and curry powder. Add hot milk and juice from salmon. Cook over low heat, stirring, for 7 to 8 minutes. Flake salmon, removing bones, and add to sauce with chopped hard-boiled eggs. Season to taste. Serve over rice.

Serves 3 to 4.

— *Janice Graham*
London, Ontario

TROUT WITH WATERCRESS

½ cup butter
4 Tbsp. finely chopped watercress
4 Tbsp. lemon juice

3 Tbsp. butter
3 Tbsp. Dijon mustard
4 lbs. trout

Combine butter, watercress and lemon juice and set aside.

Melt remaining 3 Tbsp. butter and blend in mustard. Brush trout with this mixture, place on greased rack and broil for 8 minutes on each side. Transfer to heated platter and top with butter-watercress mixture.

Serves 4.

— *Valerie Marien*
Orangeville, Ontario

PICKEREL AMERICAN STYLE

½ cup water
2 Tbsp. lemon juice
Salt & white pepper
2 lbs. pickerel, cleaned
2 Tbsp. butter
1 Tbsp. olive oil
2 shallots, chopped

1 onion, chopped
2 cloves garlic, crushed
⅛ cup Cognac
1 cup dry white wine
6 tomatoes, peeled
Cayenne
2 Tbsp. chopped parsley

Combine water, lemon juice, salt and pepper in saucepan and bring to a boil. Add fish, reduce heat and simmer for 6 to 7 minutes. Remove fish from stock, discard stock and let fish cool. When cool enough to handle, peel and remove bones and cut fish into 1-inch cubes.

Heat butter and oil and sauté shallots, onion and garlic until golden. Warm Cognac and pour over the vegetables. Flame, then add wine and simmer until reduced to half original volume.

Meanwhile, cut tomatoes into small pieces and add to sauce along with fish and cayenne. Sprinkle with parsley and serve.

Serves 4.

— *Trudi Keillor*
Berwyn, Alberta

WALTER'S WALLEYE

THE FILLETS SHOULD BE GOLDEN BROWN WITH DARKER BROWN FLECKS OF ALMONDS. IF ANY darker, the fish has been overcooked and will be dry and tasteless. This recipe can easily be prepared over a campfire or propane stove.

3 Tbsp. butter
1 clove garlic, minced
1 tsp. freshly grated ginger
½ cup slivered almonds
1½ lbs. pickerel fillets

Over low heat, melt butter and add garlic, ginger and almonds. Simmer gently for 3 minutes. Turn heat to medium, add fish fillets and fry until fish flakes easily with a fork.

Serves 4 to 6.

— *Dave Walter*
Edmonton, Alberta

STIR-FRIED COD WITH RED & GREEN

3 Tbsp. oil
6 green onions, cut in 1½-inch lengths
2-3 cloves garlic, chopped
1-inch piece fresh ginger, peeled & thinly sliced
1½ lbs. cod, cut in 1½-inch pieces
1 green pepper, thinly sliced

2-3 stalks celery, sliced diagonally
1 large onion, sliced in thin wedges
2-3 ripe tomatoes, cut into eighths
¼ cup water
¼ cup soya sauce
1 Tbsp. cornstarch or tapioca starch

Heat oil in a wok or large skillet. Add green onions, garlic and ginger, stir-fry for a minute or so until the aroma is released and the onions turn bright green. Add cod, green pepper, celery and onion, cover and steam for 4 to 5 minutes or until cod is almost cooked. A few tablespoons of water may be added if there is a danger of scorching. Add tomatoes, and cook, covered, for another 4 to 5 minutes. Mix water with soya sauce and cornstarch. Pour over cod, and cook, stirring, until it thickens. Serve immediately over rice or noodles.

Serves 4 to 6.

— *Lois Linds*
Pender Island, British Columbia

MORUE PROVENCALE

1 lb. salt cod
1 large onion, chopped
1 large clove garlic, crushed
3-4 tomatoes, chopped

Olive oil
½ tsp. basil
½ tsp. thyme
Flour

Soak cod in water for at least 24 hours, rinsing well a few times. Dry thoroughly.

Fry onion, garlic and tomatoes in olive oil for 20 minutes. Add basil and thyme.

Coat fish with flour and brown on both sides in olive oil. Add tomato sauce, cover pan and simmer until fish flakes easily — 10 to 15 minutes.

Serves 4.

— *Janet Jokinen*
Cobourg, Ontario

SMOKED FISH SAUTE

THE CONTRIBUTOR BROUGHT THE FOLLOWING AND OTHER FISH RECIPES FROM CAPE OF GOOD Hope where she spent her childhood. This recipe is adapted to Canadian taste by substituting smoked fish for barracuda.

2 lbs. smoked fish
½ cup oil
2 large onions, cut into rings
1 green pepper, chopped
3 large potatoes, peeled & sliced

Soak fish overnight in cold water. Drain, then boil in just enough water to cover until it is tender and flakes easily with a fork.

In a large skillet, heat oil and sauté onions until golden. Add green pepper and cook for 3 minutes. Set vegetables aside. Using same oil, fry potatoes until golden. Pour off excess oil, then add fish and vegetables. Cook, stirring often, until mixture is crisp and light brown. Serve with marinated tomato and onion slices and rice.

Serves 8.

— *Lucille Schur*
Toronto, Ontario

ORIENTAL STEAMED FISH

2-3 fillets of fish or small whole fish (cod, salmon,
    sturgeon, tuna)
2 slices fresh ginger, peeled & cut into thin strips
1 Tbsp. soya sauce
1 Tbsp. oil
4 green onions, chopped

Place fish in a shallow dish. Add remaining ingredients, except green onions, over fish, place in steamer and steam for approximately 15 minutes or until fish flakes easily.

Garnish fish with green onions and serve.

Serves 2.

— *Joyce Falkowski*
Gold River, British Columbia

MBISI YE KALOU NA LOSA

THIS STIR-FRY DISH CAME TO THE CONTRIBUTOR THROUGH A FRIEND, WHO OBTAINED IT IN Brazil from a woman of African descent.

1 onion, chopped	Dill weed
1 green pepper, chopped	Paprika
Olive oil	½ tsp. salt
½ lb. greens, cut into ½-inch strips (kohlrabi, collard, kale)	1 cup water
	1 lb. fish fillets, cut into finger-sized strips
Fennel	5 Tbsp. butter
Thyme	

Sauté onion and green pepper in oil for 5 minutes. Add greens, a few pinches of fennel, several of thyme, a few sprigs of dill weed, several dashes of paprika, salt and water. Cover and simmer for 5 to 10 minutes.

Add fish and butter, cover and simmer for another 20 minutes.

Serves 4.

— *Virginia Walker*
Sydenham, Ontario

FISH CAKES

WHEN THIS READER IS PREPARING MASHED POTATOES, SHE MAKES 2 OR 3 EXTRA CUPS, AS THESE fish cakes are a real favourite.

2-3 cups mashed potatoes
2 cups flaked, cooked fish fillets
4 green onions, finely chopped
2 eggs, beaten
Salt & pepper
Dash of soya sauce
Bacon fat or oil

Combine all ingredients, except oil, seasoning to taste. Heat bacon fat or oil in a skillet to a depth of ½ inch. Drop mixture by spoonfuls and fry until crispy brown on both sides.

Serve with tartar sauce or stewed tomatoes.

Serves 4 to 6.

— *Nancy Doyle*
Secaucus, New Jersey

FRIED SMELTS

2 lbs. smelts
½ cup flour
½ tsp. salt
Pepper
2 eggs

1-2 Tbsp. lemon juice
1 cup corn meal
⅓ cup grated Parmesan cheese
2 Tbsp. minced parsley
Oil for frying

Clean smelts. Combine flour, salt and pepper. Beat together eggs and lemon juice. Combine corn meal, Parmesan cheese and parsley.

Dredge smelts in flour, then dip in egg mixture, then roll in corn meal.

Fry quickly in ¼ inch of oil heated to 350 degrees F. Serve with lemon wedges.

Serves 6 to 8.

— *Lynne Roe*
Orangeville, Ontario

EULACHON

EULACHON, ALSO KNOWN AS CANDLEFISH AND OOLICHAN, IS A SMALL SMELTLIKE FISH FOUND on the Pacific coast. It is at its most abundant in early spring. As well as being delicious prepared as the recipe below indicates, eulachon can also be rendered into a pure, cream-coloured grease and used in place of vegetable oil.

6 eulachon
Butter
Fresh parsley
Lemon wedges
Pepper

Fry eulachon in butter and serve with parsley, lemon and pepper. Eat head, tail and bones.

Serves 2.

— *Karen Maxwell*
Greenville, British Columbia

LINGUINE WITH SHRIMP & GREEN PEPPER

3-4 Tbsp. oil
1-2 cloves garlic, minced
1 red onion, thinly sliced
1 green pepper, thinly sliced
Salt & pepper
Chili powder
Basil
1 cup cooked shrimp

1 tomato, chopped
2 Tbsp. parsley, finely chopped
¼ cup white wine
⅛ cup brandy
1 Tbsp. butter
8 oz. linguine
Parmesan cheese

Heat oil, add garlic, onion and green pepper, and sauté until golden brown. Add salt and pepper, chili powder, basil, shrimp, tomato and parsley. Simmer for 7 minutes. Add wine and brandy and flame briefly. Add butter and simmer for 5 minutes.

Meanwhile, cook linguine, drain, and add to skillet. Mix well and sprinkle with cheese.

Serves 4.

— Anna Sarraino
Weston, Ontario

VICKI'S BIRTHDAY SHRIMP

2 cloves garlic, minced
2 Tbsp. olive oil
½ cup white wine
1 Tbsp. basil
24 large shrimp, cleaned & shelled
1 zucchini, sliced
¼ lb. snow peas

½ lb. mushrooms
1 green pepper, sliced
½ red pepper, sliced
2 cups peeled, chopped fresh tomatoes
1-2 Tbsp. flour
8 oz. fettuccine, cooked, drained & buttered

Combine garlic, olive oil, wine and basil. Marinate shrimp in this for several hours.

Stir-fry zucchini, snow peas, mushrooms and peppers until crispy-tender. Remove from pan.

Place shrimp and marinade in pan, and cook briefly until shrimp are firm and pink. Remove shrimp with slotted spoon. Sprinkle tomatoes with flour and add to pan. Cook until thickened, add vegetables and shrimp, and heat through. Serve over fettuccine.

Serves 4.

GREENLANDIC SHRIMP FETTUCCINE

¾ lb. fettuccine
1 bunch broccoli, broken into bite-sized pieces
¾ cup butter
1 clove garlic, crushed
1 onion, chopped

½ lb. mushrooms, sliced
1 tsp. cornstarch
1 cup cream
1¼ cups Parmesan cheese
2 lbs. Greenland shrimp, cooked & shelled

Cook fettuccine and broccoli separately until just tender. Drain and set aside.

Melt 4 Tbsp. of the butter, and sauté garlic, onion and mushrooms until tender. Remove from pan and set aside. Melt remaining butter, stir in cornstarch, then cream and cheese. Cook, stirring, until hot and thickened.

Toss together fettuccine, broccoli, onion, mushrooms, sauce and shrimp, and heat through.

Serves 6.

— Wendy Dodd
Frobisher Bay, Northwest Territories

PIRAEUS SHRIMP

SERVED IN BOWLS WITH A LOAF OF ITALIAN BREAD FOR DIPPING, THIS MAKES A DELICIOUS MEAL in itself. It takes its name from the Greek port where the contributors first tasted it.

2 medium onions, chopped
3 large cloves garlic, chopped
2½ Tbsp. olive oil
28-oz. can tomatoes, lightly chopped
Oregano & basil

Salt & pepper
¼ cup white wine
1 lb. shelled, deveined shrimp
8 oz. feta cheese, crumbled

Sauté onions and garlic in oil for 30 seconds over medium-high heat. Add tomatoes, oregano, basil, salt and pepper. Cook until boiling, then add wine. Stir in shrimp when liquid is boiling. Simmer for 5 minutes, or until shrimp turn pinkish white. Add cheese and cook for another 2 or 3 minutes.

Serves 4.

— John & Elaine Bird
Toronto, Ontario

SHRIMP BASIL

¼ cup butter
1 cup chopped onion
¼ cup chopped green pepper
¼ cup chopped celery
½ cup sliced mushrooms
1 lb. shrimp, peeled & deveined
2 Tbsp. cornstarch

1 tsp. basil
¼ tsp. salt
1 cup chicken stock
2 Tbsp. white wine
1 cup cream
3 Tbsp. sour cream

Melt butter and sauté onion, green pepper, celery and mushrooms until onion is transparent — 5 minutes. Add shrimp and cook for 1 minute. Remove from heat and keep covered.

Blend cornstarch, basil and salt with chicken stock and wine in saucepan and cook over low heat, stirring, until thickened — about 2 to 3 minutes. Add shrimp and vegetables, then stir in cream and sour cream. Heat through, but do not boil.

Serve over rice or noodles.

Serves 4 to 6.

— Joanne Saunders
Mahone Bay, Nova Scotia

CREOLE JAMBALAYA A LA DAVID

½ cup butter
½ cup chopped onions
½ cup chopped celery with leaves
½ cup chopped scallions
½ cup diced ham
⅓ cup chopped green pepper
1 tsp. minced garlic

1 lb. shrimp, shelled
1½ cups beef stock
26-oz. can chopped tomatoes
Bay leaf
½ tsp. salt
¼ tsp. cayenne
1½ cups raw rice

Melt butter in large heavy saucepan. Add onions, celery, scallions, ham, green pepper and garlic and sauté until vegetables are just tender. Add shrimp and cook for 5 minutes. Add beef stock, tomatoes, bay leaf, salt and cayenne and cook over low heat for 10 to 15 minutes.

Add rice, stir well, cover and cook over very low heat for 25 to 30 minutes or until rice is tender.

Serves 4 to 6.

— David Bradley
Fort St. John, British Columbia

SHRIMP IN BEER CREOLE

½ cup sliced blanched almonds
3 Tbsp. butter
1 Tbsp. oil
Salt
2 lbs. shrimp, shelled & deveined
¼ cup butter
¼ cup minced scallions

1 green pepper, cut into strips
½ lb. small mushrooms
1 Tbsp. paprika
Salt & pepper
1 tsp. tomato paste
1 cup light beer
¾ cup heavy cream

In a small skillet, sauté almonds in 1 Tbsp. of butter and the oil until golden. Drain on paper towels, sprinkle with salt and set aside.

Cook shrimp in ¼ cup butter over medium heat, stirring, until they turn pink. Transfer shrimp and pan juices to a bowl and reserve.

Add remaining 2 Tbsp. butter to saucepan and sauté scallions and green pepper until softened. Add mushrooms, paprika, salt and pepper and cook until mushrooms are tender. Stir in tomato paste, beer and pan juices and reduce liquid over high heat to ½ cup. Reduce heat to low, add cream and shrimp and simmer until hot.

Serve over rice pilaf and garnish with almonds.

Serves 4.

— *Veronica Green*
Winnipeg, Manitoba

SHRIMP CURRY IN AVOCADO

2 Tbsp. butter
1½ tsp. curry powder
½ tsp. salt
1 tomato, chopped
2 scallions, cut on the diagonal
1½ cups small shrimp, shelled & deveined

2 Tbsp. lime juice
1 cup sour cream
Pepper
4 avocadoes, peeled, halved & sprinkled with
    lemon juice

Melt butter and add curry powder and salt. Sauté for 2 minutes, stirring constantly. Add tomato and scallions, then shrimp. Cook for 3 to 4 minutes. Stir in lime juice, sour cream and pepper to taste. Simmer gently to heat sauce, but do not boil.

Fill avocado halves with hot shrimp and serve immediately.

Serves 4.

— *Lisa Calzonetti*
Elora, Ontario

SWEET AND SOUR PAPAYA SHRIMP

THIS SEAFOOD-FRUIT COMBINATION SATISFIES THE APPETITES OF BOTH THOSE WHO ENJOY tropical fruits and those who are addicted to seafood.

3 Tbsp. butter
¾ cup chopped onion
1 papaya, peeled, seeded & puréed
¼ cup vinegar
2 Tbsp. brown sugar
1 Tbsp. lime juice

¼ tsp. dry mustard
⅛ tsp. ginger
⅛ tsp. curry powder
Pepper
Salt
1 lb. shrimp

Melt butter in Dutch oven and sauté onion until softened but not browned. Add remaining ingredients, except shrimp, and bring to a boil. Simmer for 5 minutes. Add shrimp and simmer for another 10 to 15 minutes. Serve over hot rice.

Serves 4.

— *Louise McDonald*
L'Orignal, Ontario

GUYANESE COOK-UP

MAKE THE COCONUT MILK FOR THIS RECIPE BY COMBINING 3 CUPS BOILING WATER WITH 1 CUP grated coconut – preferably fresh. When mixture is cool enough to handle, squeeze out all the liquid and discard the coconut.

1½ cups raw brown rice
3 cups coconut milk
½ tsp. salt
¾ cup sliced green beans
½ cup shrimp

Cook rice in coconut milk with salt for 25 minutes. Place green beans and shrimp on top of rice to steam for remaining cooking time – about 20 minutes. Stir when cooked and serve.

Serves 4.

— *Shiela Alexandrovich*
Whitehorse, Yukon

CHICKEN AND SHRIMP

THE CONTRIBUTOR HAS BEEN USING THIS RECIPE FOR MORE THAN 20 YEARS. HER ONE UNHAPPY experience with it resulted from serving it to her father-in-law at a birthday celebration, only to watch him swell up from an allergic reaction to the shellfish.

1 Tbsp. salt
Pepper
3½-4-lb. broiler, cut into serving-sized pieces
¼ cup butter
2 medium onions, finely chopped
1 clove garlic, minced

3 Tbsp. minced parsley
½ cup port wine
1 cup tomato sauce
1 tsp. basil
1 lb. shrimp, shelled & deveined
Parsley

An hour before serving, rub salt and pepper over chicken pieces. Melt butter in a large skillet and brown chicken on all sides. Add onions, garlic, parsley, wine, tomato sauce and basil. Simmer, covered, for 30 minutes or until chicken is tender. Push chicken to one side, bring juices to a boil, add shrimp, cover and cook for 3 to 4 minutes or until shrimp is uniformly pink. Remove chicken to a serving platter, top with shrimp. Skim fat from surface of sauce, pour over chicken and shrimp. Sprinkle with parsley.

Serves 4 to 6.

— *Connie Dingman*
Hannon, Ontario

FETTUCCINE WITH CRAB

1½ cups whipping cream
4 cups cooked fettuccine
6 oz. crabmeat
¾ cup grated Parmesan cheese
Salt & pepper
Parsley

Bring cream to a boil in skillet and boil for 1 minute or until slightly reduced. Add pasta and return to boil, then stir in crabmeat and ½ cup Parmesan cheese. Add salt and pepper to taste. Sprinkle with remaining cheese and parsley and serve.

Serves 4.

— *June Plamondon*
Moisie, Quebec

MARYLAND CRAB CAKES

1 lb. crabmeat, lightly flaked
1½ cups bread crumbs
2-3 Tbsp. minced scallions
½ Tbsp. chopped thyme

¼ cup mayonnaise
1 egg
2 tsp. Dijon mustard
2 Tbsp. butter

Toss together crabmeat, ½ cup bread crumbs, scallions and thyme.

In another bowl, combine mayonnaise, egg and mustard. Stir into crab mixture. Form into 8 patties and coat with remaining 1 cup bread crumbs.

Heat butter in large, heavy skillet and sauté patties until golden on both sides and heated through.

Serves 4.

— Nancy Doyle
Secaucus, New Jersey

CHINESE SHALLOW-FRIED NOODLES WITH SEAFOOD

½ lb. fresh vermicelli noodles
5 Tbsp. sesame oil

Topping
¼ lb. small shrimp, rinsed & shelled
¼ lb. scallops
¼ lb. abalone, cut into bite-sized
  pieces
¼ lb. chicken, shredded

Marinade
2 tsp. light soya sauce
2 tsp. dry sherry
1 egg white, well beaten
1 Tbsp. cornstarch

Vegetables
6 dried Chinese mushrooms,
  presoaked for 30 minutes

¼ cup sliced bamboo shoots
2 cups snow peas, stems
  removed & halved
1 onion, cut into small wedges

Seasonings
1½ cups chicken stock
2 Tbsp. light soya sauce
Sugar
¼ tsp. pepper

6 Tbsp. sesame oil
2 scallions, cut in 1½-inch sections
4 thin slices ginger, shredded
1½ Tbsp. cornstarch dissolved in
  2 Tbsp. water

Pour boiling water over noodles and let them sit for 15 to 20 minutes. Drain, rinse and then spread on platter or towel to dry for at least 1 hour.

Meanwhile, marinate seafood and chicken in soya sauce, sherry, egg white and cornstarch, refrigerated, for at least 30 minutes. Stir well after 15 minutes.

Heat wok, add oil and heat for 30 seconds. Add noodles, coiling into a large pancake, and fry over high heat for a few seconds. Reduce heat to medium and continue cooking for 5 minutes or until bottom is brown and crisp. Flip pancake over and cook for another 5 minutes until second side is also brown and crispy. Place on paper towelling to drain and then keep warm in oven.

Rinse, pat dry and quarter the mushrooms. Combine with remaining vegetables. Mix together chicken stock, soya sauce, sugar to taste and pepper for seasoning.

Add 4 Tbsp. oil to hot wok and heat for 30 seconds. Scatter in scallions and ginger and cook, stirring, for 30 seconds. Add vegetables and cook for 1 minute. Add seasonings and stir well. When the liquid boils, reduce heat to medium, add seafood and chicken and cook until opaque – no more than 2 minutes. Turn heat to low, add dissolved cornstarch and cook, stirring, until sauce is smooth and thick. Sprinkle in remaining 2 Tbsp. oil, stir well and pour over noodle pancake.

Serves 4.

— Gwenda Wells
Alcove, Ontario

PASTA TUTTO MARE

4 Tbsp. butter
3¾ cups light cream
1½ cups sliced mushrooms
¼ lb. mild semisoft cheese (e.g. mozzarella or brick), cubed
1 Tbsp. finely chopped parsley
1 tsp. minced garlic

1 tsp. salt
Curry powder
Pepper
8 oz. cooked crabmeat
8 oz. cooked shrimp
1 lb. small pasta shells
1½ cups Parmesan cheese

Melt butter in heavy skillet. Add cream, mushrooms, cheese, parsley, garlic, salt, curry powder and pepper. Bring to a boil over medium heat, stirring constantly. Add crabmeat, shrimp and pasta, sprinkle with Parmesan cheese, and reduce heat to low. Simmer, uncovered, stirring frequently, until slightly thickened – 2 to 3 minutes.

Serves 4 to 6.

— Lucia Cyre
Logan Lake, British Columbia

SEAFOOD CREAM CURRY

2 Tbsp. butter
1 small onion, chopped
1 clove garlic, crushed
1 tsp. minced ginger
1½ Tbsp. flour
2 Tbsp. curry powder
¼ tsp. turmeric
½ tsp. salt

1½ cups coconut milk (soak 1 cup coconut in 2 cups hot milk for ½ hour, strain)
½ cup whipping cream
¼ lb. small shrimp, cooked & shelled
¼ lb. cooked crabmeat
Lemon juice

Melt butter in heavy skillet over medium heat. Add onion, garlic and ginger and cook for 10 minutes. Combine flour, curry powder, turmeric and salt. Add to skillet and cook, stirring constantly, for 5 minutes. Gradually whisk in milk, stirring until smooth. Reduce heat to low, cover and simmer for 20 minutes, stirring occasionally.

Strain mixture into saucepan. Add cream, shrimp and crab to saucepan and stir to blend. Heat through, add lemon juice and serve.

Serves 2.

— D. Sacuta
Prince George, British Columbia

SHRIMP AND CRAB VALHALLA

4 Tbsp. butter
¼ cup chopped onion
¼ cup chopped celery
¼ cup chopped green pepper
¼ cup chopped red pepper
2 Tbsp. flour
1 cup milk
2 egg yolks

½ cup whipping cream
Salt & pepper
Tabasco sauce
⅛ tsp. ground nutmeg
¼ cup dry sherry
¾ lb. shrimp, shelled & deveined
¾ lb. crabmeat

Heat 2 Tbsp. butter in a small saucepan and sauté onion, celery and peppers for 5 minutes. Set aside. Melt remaining butter in a second saucepan, add flour and cook, stirring, over medium heat for 1 minute. Gradually whisk in milk, and cook, stirring, until thickened. Combine a few tablespoons sauce with egg yolks. Stir mixture into sauce and cook for 2 minutes. Add cream and seasonings. Stir in sherry and keep warm.

Add shrimp to vegetables, cooking until shrimp turn pink. Stir in crabmeat and add to sauce. Heat through, but do not boil.

Serve over parsleyed rice.

Serves 4.

— Heather Quiney
Victoria, British Columbia

SCALLOPS CREME DE LA CREME

A VARIATION ON THIS RECIPE IS TO PLACE THE COOKED INGREDIENTS IN SCALLOP SHELLS OR AU gratin dishes, top them with bread crumbs and Parmesan cheese and broil until golden brown.

1 lb. scallops	⅓ cup grated Gruyère cheese
½ cup milk	2 egg yolks, beaten
2 Tbsp. butter	3 Tbsp. sherry
2 Tbsp. flour	⅛ tsp. lemon pepper
2 cups whipping cream	

If scallops are much different in size, cut larger ones. Poach in milk until opaque — 5 minutes. Set aside.

Melt butter and stir in flour. Cook over medium heat for 2 minutes. Slowly stir in whipping cream and cheese. Cook, stirring, over medium heat until thickened.

Stir 2 Tbsp. of sauce into beaten egg yolks and mix well. Return egg mixture to cream sauce, stirring thoroughly. Add scallops, sherry and lemon pepper. Cook until heated through, stirring to prevent burning.

— C. Miller

Serves 4.

COLETTE'S FETTUCCINE

A SIMPLE BUT ELEGANT DISH, THIS MAKES PERFECT COMPANY FARE THAT WILL ALWAYS GET raves.

¾ cup butter	1 cup clam juice
½ lb. scallops, cut into quarters	2 cups heavy cream
1 tsp. salt	4 green onions, chopped
Pepper	4-6 cups cooked fettuccine
1 clove garlic, crushed	

Melt butter in heavy pot. Add scallops, salt, pepper and garlic. Cook over low heat until scallops are cooked — 5 minutes. Add clam juice and cream and simmer for 3 minutes. Add green onions and cook at a slow boil for another 5 minutes. If sauce is too thin, gradually stir in a little flour to thicken.

Serve over cooked, buttered fettuccine.

— Colette McFarland
Telkwa, British Columbia

Serves 2 to 3.

SCALLOPS WITH BABY CORN COBS

1 lb. scallops	¼ cup water
2 Tbsp. tapioca powder or cornstarch	2 Tbsp. oil
1 tsp. salt	2 green onions, cut in 2-inch lengths
1 Tbsp. sherry	1 clove garlic, minced
Sesame seed oil	1 tsp. minced ginger
1 tsp. sugar	14-oz. can baby corn cobs
Pepper	

Cut scallops in half and marinate in 1 Tbsp. tapioca powder, ½ tsp. salt, sherry and a few drops sesame seed oil. Set aside.

In a small bowl, make sauce by combining salt, sugar, 1 Tbsp. tapioca powder, pepper, water and a few drops sesame seed oil.

Heat 2 Tbsp. oil in wok and stir-fry green onions, garlic and ginger for 1 minute. Add scallops and stir-fry until cooked — no more than 5 minutes. Drain corn and add to scallops. Heat through, add sauce and bring to a boil. Serve immediately.

Serves 3 to 4.

— Sylvia Petz
Willowdale, Ontario

OCTOPUS SAUTE

THIS PORTUGUESE DISH IS AS SIMPLE TO PREPARE AS IT IS DELICIOUS. SERVED OVER RICE, IT IS good hot; chilled, it makes an unusual appetizer.

1 lb. octopus
6-8 cloves garlic, minced
2 Tbsp. butter
2 Tbsp. olive oil
½ cup chopped parsley

Several sprigs fresh marjoram, finely chopped
½ cup dry red wine
1-2 Tbsp. capers, chopped
Salt & pepper
1-2 tsp. ground cumin

Clean octopus, removing ink sack carefully and discarding, then cut meat into bite-sized pieces. Sauté garlic in butter and oil for 3 minutes. Add octopus, parsley and marjoram, barely cover with wine, cover pot and simmer gently until octopus pieces curl and turn pinkish. This will take 10 to 15 minutes. Add capers. Do not overcook, as octopus will become tough. Season with salt, pepper and cumin.

Serves 4.

— *Deborah Washington*
Bath, Ontario

CALAMARI LINGUINE

CALAMARI (DERIVED FROM THE LATIN WORD FOR PEN) ARE PEN-SHAPED SQUID ABOUT 6 INCHES in length. They should be cleaned and left to develop texture and flavour for 12 hours before cooking.

1 Tbsp. olive oil
1 large onion, sliced
6 cloves garlic, minced
1½ lbs. calamari, cut into bite-sized pieces
2 cups canned tomatoes
2 tsp. salt

¼ tsp. pepper
Tabasco sauce
¼ tsp. oregano
⅛ tsp. basil
8 oz. hot cooked linguine
2 Tbsp. chopped parsley

Heat oil and sauté onion and garlic until tender. Add calamari and cook, stirring, until no longer moist. Add tomatoes, salt, pepper, Tabasco sauce, oregano and basil, and simmer for 1 hour.

Pour sauce over linguine, garnish with parsley and serve.

Serves 4.

— *Heather Quiney*
Victoria, British Columbia

LINGUINE WITH MUSHROOM & CLAM SAUCE

EITHER REGULAR OR SPINACH LINGUINE CAN BE USED IN THIS RECIPE.

8 oz. linguine
1 Tbsp. butter
2 cups sliced mushrooms
¼ cup sliced green onions
2 cloves garlic, minced

½ cup light cream
¼ cup white wine
12-oz. can clams, drained
2 Tbsp. chopped parsley
2 Tbsp. Parmesan cheese

Cook linguine until just tender, drain and rinse. Heat butter in large skillet, and sauté mushrooms, onions and garlic until tender. Add cream and wine, and simmer for 1 minute. Add clams and parsley, and simmer for 3 minutes more.

Pour sauce over linguine and toss. Sprinkle with Parmesan cheese and serve.

Serves 4.

— *Cinda Chavich*
Saskatoon, Saskatchewan

SPINACH LINGUINE WITH RED CLAM SAUCE

FRESH PASTA, EASILY MADE AT HOME AND INCREASINGLY AVAILABLE IN SPECIALTY STORES, offers a flavour and texture that is far superior to commercial dried noodles. The pasta becomes an integral part of the dish, not just the base for the sauce. Fresh pasta, with a cooking time of less than 5 minutes, is strongly recommended for this recipe.

2 Tbsp. olive oil
2 cloves garlic, minced
1 small onion, chopped
1 tsp. chopped fresh marjoram
1 tsp. chopped fresh basil
3 tomatoes, peeled & chopped

1 Tbsp. tomato paste
4 Tbsp. dry white wine
10-oz. can baby clams
½ lb. spinach linguine
Parmesan cheese

Heat olive oil in heavy pot, and sauté garlic and onion for 5 minutes. Add marjoram and basil, and sauté for 2 more minutes. Stir in tomatoes, tomato paste, wine and clams; cover and simmer for 20 minutes.

Cook linguine until just tender. Drain, rinse under hot water, and serve immediately with clam sauce. Top with Parmesan cheese.

Serves 4.

— *Jane Pugh*
Toronto, Ontario

CLAM SAUCE FOR SPAGHETTI

¼ cup butter
5 cloves garlic, peeled & halved
2 Tbsp. whole wheat flour
2 Tbsp. powdered milk
10-oz. can whole baby butter clams
Oregano
6 oz. spaghetti, cooked

Melt butter and slowly sauté garlic for 3 minutes. Do not let butter brown. Remove garlic and add flour and milk. Blend well and remove from heat.

Drain clams and add liquid to flour mixture slowly, beating well with a whisk. Return sauce to medium heat, and cook for about 4 minutes or until thick. Add clams and oregano, and pour over spaghetti.

Serves 2.

— *Linda Townsend*
Nanaimo, British Columbia

CLAM CHILI

24-30 littleneck steamer clams or butter clams, steamed & cleaned
1 cup reserved clam juice
2 26-oz. cans crushed tomatoes
7-oz. can tomato paste
½ lb. mushrooms, sliced

1 onion, sliced
1-3 tsp. chili powder
½ tsp. cayenne or 3 jalapeño peppers, seeded & chopped
2 16-oz. cans kidney beans

Combine all ingredients in heavy pot and simmer for 1 to 2 hours, stirring frequently.

Serves 8.

— *Lois Linds*
Pender Island, British Columbia

POACHED SALMON WITH MUSTARD CAPER SAUCE

4 salmon steaks
4 lemon slices
1 cup chicken stock
¼ cup white wine
White pepper

2 tsp. cornstarch
2 Tbsp. water
1 egg yolk, beaten
2 tsp. capers
1 tsp. Dijon mustard

Place salmon in lightly greased skillet with lemon slices on top. Combine chicken stock, wine and pepper and pour over salmon. Cover and simmer for 5 to 10 minutes or until fish flakes easily. Remove lemon slices and fish from skillet. Set aside and keep warm.

Boil stock mixture gently for 5 minutes or until reduced to ¾ cup. Dissolve cornstarch in water and stir into stock. Cook, stirring, until thickened and bubbling. Cook for 1 minute longer. Gradually stir half the hot mixture into the egg yolk, then return to skillet. Cook for 2 minutes. Stir in capers and mustard and heat through.

Place salmon on serving platter, spoon sauce over salmon and serve.

Serves 4.

— Joyce Falkowski
Gold River, British Columbia

PAN-FRIED OYSTERS

½ cup fine cracker crumbs
¼ cup flour
¼ tsp. salt
¼ tsp. pepper

12 oysters, drained
2 eggs, beaten
Oil

Combine cracker crumbs, flour, salt and pepper. Dip oysters in beaten eggs, then in crumb mixture.

Heat oil in skillet. Fry oysters until golden brown on both sides. Serve at once.

Serves 2 as an appetizer.

— Frieda Meding
Trochu, Alberta

ORIENTAL SQUID

6-8 squid
4 Tbsp. sesame oil
2-3 slices ginger
2-3 cloves garlic, crushed
1 carrot, sliced diagonally
1 green pepper, cut into strips
1 onion, sliced
1 small head Bok Choy,
  sliced diagonally

1 small head Siew Choy,
  leaves separated
1 cup sliced mushrooms
Soya sauce
Oyster sauce
2 Tbsp. cornstarch dissolved in
  ¼ cup water

Prepare squid by removing backbone and head. Cut body into ½-inch rings, discarding entrails.

Heat wok, add oil and heat for 30 seconds. Add half the ginger and garlic and cook for 1 to 2 minutes. Add squid, carrot, pepper and onion and cook for another 3 minutes, stirring. Add Bok Choy and Siew Choy, stir well, add ½ cup water, cover and steam for 2 minutes. Remove lid, add remaining ginger and garlic and cook for 1 minute. Add mushrooms and soya and oyster sauces. Cook for 3 minutes. Stir in dissolved cornstarch and cook, stirring, until sauce thickens.

Serves 4.

— R. Devos
Inuvik, Northwest Territories

SOUR CREAM TROUT

4 trout
Salt
½ cup flour
2 Tbsp. oil
2 Tbsp. butter

Sauce
2 Tbsp. butter
1 cup sour cream
½ tsp. lemon juice

Clean fish, but do not remove heads or tails. Dry inside and out and sprinkle cavities with salt. Coat fish with flour, shaking off excess.

In heavy skillet, heat oil and butter, lowering heat to medium after foam subsides. Fry trout two at a time, about 5 minutes per side. When browned, keep warm in 200-degree-F oven while preparing sauce.

Drain fat from skillet in which trout was cooked, but leave drippings. Melt butter and cook over low heat, stirring and scraping drippings with wooden spoon. Add sour cream and cook for 3 minutes longer, stirring, without boiling, then mix in lemon juice. Pour over hot fish and serve.

Serves 4.

— Kathy Payette
Kitchener, Ontario

OYSTERS WITH GINGER AND ONIONS

2 Tbsp. oyster sauce
1 Tbsp. cornstarch
1 tsp. sugar
1 Tbsp. soya sauce
Sesame oil
¼ cup water

3 Tbsp. oil
1 inch fresh ginger, peeled & thinly sliced
1 medium onion, thinly sliced
3-4 green onions, cut into 1-to 2-inch pieces, white & green parts separated
1 lb. oysters, drained

Mix together oyster sauce, cornstarch, sugar, soya sauce, sesame oil and water in a small bowl. Heat oil until very hot, then add ginger, onion and white parts of green onions. Cook briefly, stirring. Add oysters, cover and cook for 2 minutes. Stir in sauce and tops of green onions. Bring to a boil and cook for 2 minutes or until slightly thickened. Serve hot over rice.

Serves 4.

— R. Hildred
Lasqueti Island, British Columbia

SHRIMP WITH GINGER & CHILIES

12 Tbsp. soya sauce
6 Tbsp. honey
2-inch piece ginger, finely chopped
3 cloves garlic, crushed
Sesame oil
½ cup chopped peanuts
Dried chili peppers, chopped
    (the amount depends entirely on
    personal taste)

1 large onion, cut into rings
1 zucchini, sliced
1 cup broccoli, broken into florets
1-2 lbs. shrimp, shelled
3 cups snow peas
1½ cups sliced mushrooms
2-3 Tbsp. cornstarch dissolved in
    ½ cup water

Combine soya sauce, honey, ginger and garlic, pour over shrimp; let sit for 30 minutes.

Heat enough oil to stir-fry the vegetables in wok. Add peanuts and cook rapidly, stirring, until they brown. Add chili peppers and cook for another 1 to 2 minutes. Reduce heat to medium and add onion. Stir-fry for 2 to 3 minutes, or until onion begins to go limp. Add zucchini and broccoli and cook for another 3 minutes. Add enough water to allow vegetables to steam. Cover and cook over medium heat for 5 minutes. Remove cover and add shrimp and marinade, snow peas and mushrooms. Cook until shrimp are pink and peas are bright green — 3 to 5 minutes. Stir in cornstarch dissolved in water, and cook, stirring, until sauce thickens.

Serves 6.

SUSHI

IN THE POPULAR MIND, SUSHI IS OFTEN EQUATED WITH RAW JAPANESE FISH DISHES, BUT IN FACT, sushi is the cooked, cooled rice dressed with flavoured vinegar for which the uncooked fish, vegetables and seaweed are served as garnishes. This recipe makes attractive wheels of rice, seafood and mushrooms encased in a thin wrapping of black seaweed (nori).

Rice
2½ cups short-grain rice
2½ cups cold water
4 Tbsp. rice vinegar or mild white
    vinegar
3 Tbsp. sugar
2½ tsp. salt
2 Tbsp. mirin (rice wine)
    or dry sherry

Seafood
4 dried mushrooms
2 Tbsp. Japanese soya sauce
1 Tbsp. sugar
2 eggs

¼ tsp. salt
1 tsp. vegetable oil
4 oz. raw tuna or 8 large shrimp,
    cooked, shelled & deveined
2 tsp. lemon juice mixed with ¼ tsp.
    dry mustard or 1 tsp. wasabi
    (powdered green horseradish)
1 cucumber, peeled & cut into strips
1 piece pickled horseradish (takuan),
    cut into 3 thin strips
6 sheets nori

Wash rice several times. Drain for 30 minutes, then put in saucepan with water. Bring to a boil, cover, turn heat to low, and cook for 15 minutes. Remove from heat, let stand, covered, for 10 minutes.

To make dressing, mix remaining rice ingredients, stirring to dissolve sugar. Pour over rice, mix gently, and cool to room temperature.

Soak mushrooms in hot water for 20 minutes. Remove stems, slice caps thinly, and simmer in ½ cup soaking liquid with soya sauce and sugar until liquid has almost evaporated.

Beat eggs with salt. Heat oil in frying pan, add eggs, and cook until just dry. Cut into thin strips.

Smear tuna (cut into strips) or shrimp with lemon-mustard mixture or wasabi.

Combine mushrooms, eggs, tuna (or shrimp), cucumber and takuan.

Put one sheet of nori on a clean napkin. Spread a sixth of the rice over two-thirds of the sheet, leaving the third farthest from you free. Place tuna mixture down the centre of the rice. Roll up the sushi, using the napkin to apply even pressure to the roll. Let the rolls rest 15 minutes before cutting into 1½-inch slices. Serve cold.

Serves 6.

Baking & Stuffing

And she made him a feast at his earnest wish of
eggs and buttercups fried with fish; –

– Edward Lear

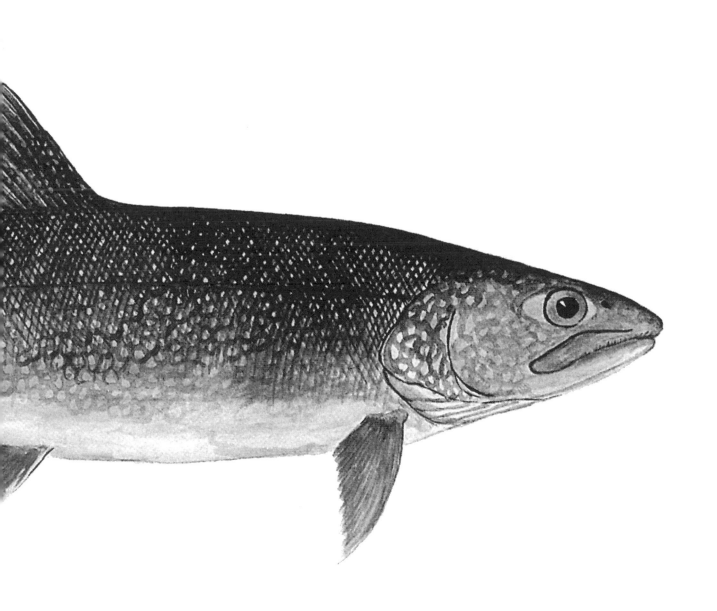

LEAHFISH WITH BERCY SAUCE

LEAH ERRINGTON, A WONDERFUL COOK AND TALENTED CERAMICIST WHO LIVES IN VANCOUVER, prepared this dish under the name "Sole and Oysters," for the contributor and her husband. They were so impressed that they now often present it to company under its new, well-deserved name.

1 lb. fresh spinach or chard
¼ tsp. nutmeg
1½ lbs. sole fillets
16 oysters (approx.)
2-3 large cloves garlic, minced
¼ cup butter
1 lemon, thinly sliced
1 onion, thinly sliced & sautéed
Parsley

Bercy Sauce
1 tsp. flour
3 Tbsp. butter
½ cup dry white wine

Wash, chop and steam spinach or chard. Lay on bottom of shallow greased baking dish and sprinkle with nutmeg.

Sauté sole, oysters and garlic in butter until sole and oysters are cooked. Reserve pan juices for sauce. Place sole on spinach and arrange oysters around it.

Make Bercy Sauce by creaming together flour and 2 Tbsp. butter. Melt remaining butter, stir in wine and pan juices, and simmer until reduced by half. Stir in flour/butter mixture.

Cover fish with Bercy Sauce and garnish with lemon slices and sautéed onion, laid alternately down the centre of the fish. Sprinkle with chopped parsley.

Bake at 400 degrees F for 10 minutes or until bubbly hot.

Serves 6.

— Jennifer Bennett
Verona, Ontario

SOLE IN LEMON PARSLEY SAUCE

2 lbs. sole fillets
½ cup butter
2 Tbsp. cornstarch
3 Tbsp. lemon juice

2 Tbsp. parsley
¼ cup finely chopped celery
Pepper

Melt butter in glass baking dish. Blend in cornstarch, lemon juice, parsley, celery and pepper.

Coat each fillet with seasoned butter and arrange in baking dish. Cover with aluminum foil.

Bake at 325 degrees F for 25 to 30 minutes.

Serves 6.

— Nancy Blenkinsop
Corbyville, Ontario

MOIRA'S POISSON AUX OEUFS

1 lb. fish fillets (cod, red snapper, sole)
2-3 eggs
¼ cup milk

½ cup grated Cheddar cheese
1 tsp. marjoram, basil or thyme
Salt & pepper

Place fillets in greased 9" x 9" baking dish. Combine remaining ingredients and pour over fish. Bake at 350 degrees F for 20 to 30 minutes or until fish flakes easily and egg mixture is puffy and golden brown.

Serves 4.

— Wendy Vine
Ganges, British Columbia

SCANDINAVIAN BAKED FISH

1 lb. fish fillets (cod, bluefish or sole)
Salt & pepper
½ tsp. dried dill
½ cup buttermilk or yogurt
1 bay leaf, crumbled

1 clove, crushed
4 peppercorns, crushed
1 clove garlic, crushed
1 Tbsp. grated onion

Place fish in a single layer on a greased baking dish. Sprinkle lightly with salt, pepper and dill. Mix buttermilk or yogurt with bay leaf, clove, peppercorns, garlic and onion. Pour mixture over fish. Bake at 375 degrees F for 20 minutes or until fish flakes easily with a fork.

Serves 4.

— Beth Killing
Midland, Ontario

WEST AFRICAN EGGPLANT AND FISH BAKE

1 cup beef stock
1 onion, thinly sliced
1 medium eggplant, cubed
2 medium zucchini, cut into 1-inch slices
1 green pepper, chopped
1-2 cloves garlic, crushed

1 tsp. tarragon
1 tsp. salt
¼ tsp. pepper
28-oz. can tomatoes, drained & chopped
1 lb. sole fillets
½ lb. cooked shrimp

Heat stock in a large saucepan, then add onion and eggplant. Cook over medium heat until tender, then add remaining vegetables and seasonings. Cover and cook for 10 minutes, stirring occasionally. Pour into a shallow casserole dish, arrange fish on top of vegetables and bake at 350 degrees F, uncovered, for 20 minutes. Add shrimp to casserole, then bake for another 5 minutes or until fish flakes easily with a fork and shrimp are heated through. Serve with rice.

— Holly Andrews
Puslinch, Ontario

BAKED FISH WITH CUCUMBER

1 lb. fish fillets (sole, haddock, turbot)
¼ cup sour cream
¼ tsp. Dijon mustard

2 Tbsp. chopped fresh dill
Salt & pepper
1 cucumber, peeled

Divide the fish into individual servings and place each serving on a piece of tin foil long enough to wrap around it comfortably.

Mix the sour cream, mustard and dill together, add salt and pepper to taste and spread the mixture over the fish. Slice the cucumber into long thin strips and divide equally onto the fish.

Seal the foil, place in baking dish and bake at 425 degrees F for 10 to 12 minutes or until fish flakes easily.

Serves 2.

— Ms Bruce Blakemore
Cape Negro, Nova Scotia

TURBOT JARDINIERE

2 lb. turbot fillets, fresh or frozen
Salt & pepper
3 Tbsp. melted butter
1 cup julienned carrots
¾ cup finely sliced green onions

1 cup sliced mushrooms
1 tomato, diced
1 Tbsp. lemon juice
2 Tbsp. dry white wine

Place fillets in greased baking dish. Season with salt and pepper and 1 Tbsp. melted butter. Bake at 450 degrees F for 5 minutes if fish is fresh and 10 minutes if it is frozen.

Heat remaining butter and sauté carrots for 2 minutes, then add remaining vegetables and cook for 1 minute longer. Place over fish and sprinkle with lemon juice and wine.

Bake at 450 degrees F, basting with pan juices for 5 to 10 minutes, or until fish flakes easily.

Serves 4.

— Ms Bruce Blakemore
Cape Negro, Nova Scotia

BAKED ROCK COD WITH BLACK BEAN SAUCE

2-4 lb. rock cod, cleaned & scaled
1 large carrot, grated
1 large onion, sliced

Black Bean Sauce
5½-oz. can Chinese salted black beans
¼ cup soya sauce

¼ cup red or white wine
¼ cup water
2 Tbsp. brown sugar
2-3 cloves garlic, finely chopped

Place cod on top of carrot and onion on foil. Set aside.

Rinse and drain beans thoroughly and mash in small bowl. Add soya sauce, wine, water, sugar and garlic and stir until well mixed. Pour over cod and seal tin foil. Bake at 425 degrees F for 10 minutes per inch of thickness.

Serves 2 to 4.

— Lois Linds
Pender Island, British Columbia

BAKED COD SUPREME

2 lbs. cod
2 cups white wine
1 cup water
1 small onion, chopped
½ tsp. oregano
3 cups peas
2 Tbsp. butter
2 Tbsp. flour

⅓ tsp. salt
Pepper
½ cup whipping cream
3 Tbsp. sherry
½ cup grated Swiss cheese
1 lb. shrimp, cooked & shelled
Buttered bread crumbs

Boil cod slowly in wine and water with onion and oregano until tender — 7 to 10 minutes. Strain cooking liquid and reserve for later use.

Butter a 9" x 13" baking dish. Spread peas in bottom and place cod on top. Melt butter and stir in flour, salt and pepper until smooth. Gradually add cream and enough reserved cooking liquid to make 1½ cups. Cook, stirring continuously, until sauce is thickened and creamy. Add sherry, cheese and shrimp and pour over cod. Top with bread crumbs and bake at 350 degrees F for 20 minutes or until heated through and browned on top.

Serves 8.

— Louise Ogloend
Hjelmeland, Norway

SWORDFISH DELRAY

2 lbs. swordfish
½ cup white wine
1 cup sour cream
1 cup mayonnaise

4 green onions, chopped
Parmesan cheese
Lemon
Parsley

Marinate fish in wine in baking dish for 30 minutes. Meanwhile, combine sour cream and mayonnaise with chopped green onions.

Drain most of the wine from the fish, leaving just enough to coat the bottom of the baking dish. Spoon sour cream and mayonnaise topping over the fish and bake at 350 degrees F for 15 minutes, covered. Remove cover, sprinkle with Parmesan cheese and bake for another 15 minutes or until top is golden brown.

Garnish with lemon and parsley and serve with buttered pasta.

Serves 4.

— *Audrey Alley*
Victoria, British Columbia

CHIARD A LA TRUITE

THIS IS A TRADITIONAL FRENCH CANADIAN RECIPE. THE QUEBECOIS FROM THE LOWER ST. Lawrence River region call it "chiard" and the Acadians call it "fricot." It can be made with a variety of meats, game and fish. *"Herbes salées"* are, literally, salted herbs, usually a mixture of green onions and parsley in pickling salt — minced parsley and green onions, without the pickling salt, make a good substitute.

¼ cup diced salt pork
1 onion, diced
2 cups water
3 cups sliced potatoes

Salt & pepper
2 Tbsp. *herbes salées* or equivalent
8-12 small trout

Fry salt pork in large ovenproof pot until it is almost crispy. Add onions and fry until golden. Add water, potatoes and seasonings, cover and cook for 15 minutes or until potatoes are tender. If necessary, add more water. Lay trout on top of potatoes and bake at 350 degrees F for 15 minutes or until fish flakes.

Serves 4 to 6.

— *Anne Levesque*
Inverness, Nova Scotia

BAKED FISH CREOLE

½ cup chopped onion
½ cup chopped celery
½ cup diced green pepper
½ cup sliced mushrooms
¼ cup sliced black olives

1 large clove garlic, crushed
1 Tbsp. oil
1 lb. fish fillets
14-oz. can tomatoes
½ cup grated Monterey Jack cheese

Sauté vegetables except tomatoes in oil until limp. Add tomatoes and their liquid, cover and simmer for 20 minutes. Spread fillets in a single layer in greased casserole dish and cover with sauce. Sprinkle with cheese and bake at 400 degrees F for 15 minutes or until fillets are tender and flake easily.

Serves 4.

— *Shelley Townsend*
Lethbridge, Alberta

SKATE

1½ lbs. skate
1 onion, chopped
1 clove garlic, chopped
½ green pepper, chopped
½ cup chopped mushrooms
2 Tbsp. oil
2 Tbsp. basil

1 Tbsp. oregano
6½-oz. can tomato paste
12-oz. can tomatoes
½ tsp. Worcestershire sauce
1 cup cooked spinach
½ cup grated Swiss cheese

Cover skate with water, bring to a boil and simmer for 10 minutes. Let cool.

Sauté onion, garlic, green pepper and mushrooms in oil. Add basil, oregano, tomato paste, tomatoes and Worcestershire sauce and simmer together for 15 minutes.

Slip the flesh of the skate off the cartilage, cut it into pieces and place in a casserole dish.

Layer spinach and ¼ cup cheese over the fish, pour the sauce over this, then top with remaining cheese.

Bake at 350 degrees F for 30 minutes.

Serves 4.

— R. Hildred
Lasqueti Island, British Columbia

DEVILLED FISH

2 lbs. fish fillets (haddock, flounder, mullet or
    ocean perch)
2 Tbsp. lemon juice
½ cup grated Parmesan cheese
½ cup sour cream
¼ cup butter, softened

3 Tbsp. mayonnaise
¼ cup chopped scallions
¼ tsp. salt
Pepper
Hot pepper sauce

Separate fish into fillets and drain well on paper towels. Place in single layer in well-greased casserole dish. Brush with lemon juice and let stand for 10 minutes.

In medium bowl, combine cheese, sour cream, butter, mayonnaise, scallions, salt, pepper and hot pepper sauce. Stir briskly until well mixed, then set aside.

Broil fish four inches from flame for five to six minutes or until fish flakes easily. Remove from broiler and spread with sauce. Return to oven and broil for two to four minutes more, until lightly browned.

Serves 6.

— Nan Millette
Corunna, Ontario

SMOKED FISH IN TOMATO SAUCE

2 lbs. smoked fish (halibut or cod)
¼ cup chopped onion
¼ cup butter
¼ cup flour

1 tsp. sugar
⅛ tsp. pepper
19-oz. can tomatoes
Spice bag of 6 peppercorns & 1 bay leaf

Cut fillets into serving-sized portions and place in greased baking pan.

Cook onion in butter until tender, then blend in flour and cook until bubbly. Add sugar and pepper. Slowly add tomatoes and cook, stirring, until thickened. Add spice bag and cook for another 5 minutes. Remove spice bag.

Pour sauce over fish and bake at 450 degrees F, allowing 10 minutes cooking time per inch thickness for fresh fish and 20 minutes for frozen fish.

Serves 6.

— Judy Koster
Bridgewater, Nova Scotia

PARRY SOUND SMELTS BAKED IN WINE

12-14 smelts
¼ cup finely grated carrot
½ cup chopped celery
2 tsp. chopped parsley
½ cup white wine

½ cup fine bread crumbs
¼ tsp. pepper
Salt
7 Tbsp. butter

Clean smelts and remove heads and tails. Sprinkle carrots, celery and parsley in baking dish and lay smelts on top. Add wine, bread crumbs, salt and pepper. Dot with butter.

Bake at 475 degrees F for 12 minutes, basting with liquid from dish.

Serves 2.

— Geraldine Horton
Lansdowne, Ontario

SHAD ROE WITH HERBS

THIS IS A SPRING DISH, AS THAT IS THE ONLY TIME THAT SHAD ROE IS GENERALLY AVAILABLE. IT also takes advantage of the earliest fresh herbs.

4 pair shad roe
3 Tbsp. butter, melted
3 Tbsp. minced parsley

3 Tbsp. minced chives
2 Tbsp. minced chervil
2 Tbsp. minced tarragon

Rinse roe and remove centre tissue dividing each pair, being careful not to tear the roe.

Brush a baking dish large enough to hold the roe in a single layer with melted butter, then sprinkle half the herbs in the pan.

Arrange roe on top of herbs, sprinkle with remaining herbs and pour remaining butter over top. Bake at 400 degrees F for 15 to 20 minutes.

Serves 4.

— Nancy Doyle
Secaucus, New Jersey

BASQUE TUNA CASSEROLE

THIS SAVORY SPANISH CASSEROLE IS BASED ON A DISH OFFERED IN THE BASQUE RESTAURANT Guria in Barcelona.

2 Tbsp. olive oil
1 onion, chopped
1 clove garlic, minced
4 slices bread, toasted
2 hard-cooked eggs
1 cup water
⅓ cup dry white wine
⅛ tsp. Tabasco sauce

2 7-oz. cans tuna, drained
¼ cup chopped almonds
¼ cup chopped stuffed olives
2 Tbsp. chopped parsley
½ cup grated Swiss or Gruyère cheese
Whole almonds
Parsley

Heat oil and sauté onion and garlic until soft but not brown.

In a blender, combine toast, eggs, water, wine and Tabasco sauce. Blend until smooth — about 1 minute.

In a large bowl, break up tuna, then add blender contents, sautéed onion, chopped almonds, olives, parsley and half the cheese. Mix well.

Spoon mixture into a 1-quart casserole dish. Sprinkle with remaining cheese, then bake at 350 degrees F for 30 minutes. Garnish with whole almonds and parsley.

Serves 4.

— Heather Quiney
Victoria, British Columbia

SALMON CROQUETTES

CROQUETTES ARE SMALL, EGG-SHAPED BALLS WHICH ARE GENERALLY DEEP FRIED. IN THIS RECIPE, however, they are baked, which produces a lighter, healthier dish. Serve with tartar sauce or sour cream as an hors d'oeuvres, or on a bed of rice with a salad as a main course.

16-oz. can salmon
1 cup fresh bread crumbs
½ cup wheat germ
4 Tbsp. mayonnaise
¼ cup milk or yogurt

1 small onion, minced
2 tsp. lemon juice
½ tsp. salt
¼ tsp. pepper
Wheat germ to roll the croquettes in

Drain salmon liquid into medium-sized bowl. Add bread crumbs and wheat germ and mix well. Stir in mayonnaise, milk, onion, lemon juice, salt, pepper and salmon and mix well.

Sprinkle some wheat germ on a plate. Shape salmon mixture into croquettes and roll in wheat germ. Place on cookie sheet and bake at 375 degrees F for 20 minutes.

Makes 16 croquettes.

— Lois Pope
Whitehorse, Yukon

BEACH BAKED CLAMS

Place desired quantity of freshly dug littleneck or butter clams on grill over open campfire. Bake until shells pop open. If clams are large, leave them on the fire for another minute or two. Serve plain, in their own juice, or accompanied by garlic butter and crusty bread.

Clams can also be cooked this way on a barbecue — the key to success here is the freshness of the clams.

— Carol Swann Jacob
Port McNeill, British Columbia

RIGHT OFF THE BOAT

FIRST DEVELOPED BY THE CONTRIBUTOR WITH SEAFOOD FRESHLY CAUGHT IN THE GULF OF Mexico near St. Petersburg, Florida, this recipe can be adapted to make use of lobster and scallops.

1 small red onion, finely diced
1 green pepper, seeded & chopped
½ lb. crabmeat
1 lb. shrimp
1 cup finely sliced celery
1 cup grated medium Cheddar cheese
½ tsp. salt
¼ tsp. dry mustard
¼ tsp. black pepper

1 Tbsp. Worcestershire sauce
Grated rind of 1 lemon
Red pepper flakes
1 cup mayonnaise
Bread crumbs
Butter
Paprika
Parsley

Combine all ingredients except bread crumbs, butter, paprika and parsley, in casserole dish and mix thoroughly to coat seafood. Sprinkle with bread crumbs, dot with butter, paprika and parsley, and bake at 300 degrees F for 30 minutes.

Serves 6 to 8.

— J.W. Houston
Willowdale, Ontario

BAKED CLAMS

1 small green pepper, chopped
1 small onion, chopped
1 stalk celery, chopped
2 Tbsp. butter
2 5-oz. cans clams, or 2 dozen fresh
½ cup fine bread crumbs

4 slices bacon, cooked & chopped
½ cup clam juice, reserved from cans
 or from clams when opened
Salt
½ tsp. thyme
Paprika

Sauté vegetables in butter, remove from heat and place in bowl. Drain clams, reserving juice, and finely chop. Add to vegetables, mix in bread crumbs, bacon, reserved clam juice, salt and thyme.

Press into greased shallow casserole dish or back into clam shells if fresh clams were used. Sprinkle with paprika and bake at 375 degrees F for 20 to 30 minutes or until browned.

Serves 6.

— Marilyn Gventer
Kingston, Ontario

BAKED LOBSTER MAIKAI

6 lobster tails
2 cups sake or dry white wine
Salt
½ cup butter
½ cup diced water chestnuts
½ cup diced bamboo shoots
½ cup diced romaine lettuce

½ cup diced celery
5 Tbsp. chili sauce
2 Tbsp. chopped parsley
1 Tbsp. chopped chives
1 tsp. Worcestershire sauce
1½ cups mayonnaise
½ cup chili sauce

Remove lobster tails from shell, dice, and marinate for 1 hour in sake or white wine and salt. Drain, then sauté in butter for 10 to 15 minutes.

Combine water chestnuts, bamboo shoots, romaine lettuce, celery, 5 Tbsp. chili sauce, parsley, chives and Worcestershire sauce in a bowl. Add cooked lobster, mix well and fill lobster shells.

Combine mayonnaise and remaining ½ cup chili sauce and pour over the stuffed lobster tails. Bake at 400 degrees F until browned — about 10 minutes.

Serves 3 to 4.

— Helen Shepherd
Lansdowne, Ontario

SHRIMP A LA GRECQUE

4 Tbsp. olive oil
2 cloves garlic, minced
2 cups chopped fresh tomatoes
½ cup white wine
¼ tsp. basil

¼ tsp. oregano
Salt & pepper
1½ lbs. shrimp, cleaned & deveined
½ lb. crumbled feta cheese

Heat 2 Tbsp. oil and briefly sauté garlic. Add tomatoes and cook, stirring, for 1 minute. Add wine, basil, oregano and salt and pepper. Simmer for 10 minutes.

In casserole dish, heat remaining 2 Tbsp. oil and sauté shrimp for one minute. Top with feta cheese and spoon tomato sauce over the cheese. Bake at 400 degrees F for 10 minutes.

Serves 4.

— Ms Bruce Blakemore
Cape Negro, Nova Scotia

STUFFED SNAPPER WITH ORANGE & LIME

4 Tbsp. butter
5 oz. shrimp, sliced
1 cup sliced mushrooms
2 green onions, finely chopped
2 stalks celery, chopped
½ tsp. tarragon
½ tsp. basil
½ tsp. thyme

1 pineapple, half sliced & half diced
5-6 lbs. red snapper fillets
Juice of 1 lime
Juice & zest of 3 oranges
2 Tbsp. flour
1 cup whipping cream
2 Tbsp. sherry
Pepper

Melt 2 Tbsp. butter and sauté shrimp, mushrooms, green onions, celery and herbs. Add diced half of pineapple and sauté for 2 to 3 minutes.

Lay fillets flat and make a slit lengthwise down the centre of each, starting and ending 2 inches from either end and being careful not to cut all the way through. Run knife sideways down the slit out towards the edges of the fillets, creating a pocket. Stuff sautéed mixture into snapper, reserving ¼ cup. Cover with lime and orange juices. Bake, covered, at 350 degrees F for 30 minutes.

Gently mince the reserved stuffing and set aside. Place remaining 2 Tbsp. butter in skillet, add flour and cook until blended. Add cream, stirring until thickened and add reserved stuffing. Stir in sherry, pepper and grated orange zest.

When snapper is cooked, remove from pan to serving dish. Add pan liquid to sauce and reduce by simmering. Surround fish with sliced pineapple and pour sauce over top.

Serves 6 to 8.

— Jan van der Est
Vancouver, British Columbia

STUFFED LOBSTER TAILS

4 lobster tails
4 oz. shrimp, peeled & deveined
4 oz. crabmeat
4 oz. scallops
⅔ cup sliced mushrooms
6 Tbsp. butter
2 Tbsp. brandy

3 Tbsp. flour
Paprika
Cayenne
1½ cups milk
¼ cup white wine
⅓ cup grated Parmesan cheese

Remove meat from lobster tails, reserving shells. Cut meat into bite-sized pieces.

Cook lobster, shrimp, crab, scallops and mushrooms in 4 Tbsp. butter for 5 minutes or until shrimp turns pink. Remove from heat, add brandy and flame.

Melt remaining 2 Tbsp. butter, stir in flour, paprika and cayenne and cook over low heat for 2 minutes. Gradually stir in milk and cook, stirring, until thickened. Add white wine.

After flame on seafood dies out, stir in white sauce and heat through. Spoon mixture into lobster shells and sprinkle with Parmesan cheese.

Broil 4 to 5 inches from heat for 2 to 3 minutes or until lightly browned.

Serves 4.

— Jane Lewis
Grand River, Nova Scotia

BAKED SALMON WITH SMOKED OYSTER DRESSING

THIS RECIPE MAKES AN ELEGANT, BUT EASILY PREPARED, DISH THAT CAN BE EITHER BAKED OR barbecued.

1 onion
1 stalk celery
½ green pepper
6 small mushrooms
1 can smoked oysters
1½-2 cups cooked brown rice

1 clove garlic, crushed
1 Tbsp. chopped parsley
½ tsp. ginger
Salt & pepper
4-5 lb. whole salmon, cleaned
1 lemon, thinly sliced

Chop onion, celery and green pepper. Slice mushrooms thinly. Chop oysters, reserving oil.

Combine rice, onion, pepper, celery, mushrooms, oysters and reserved oil, garlic, parsley, ginger and salt and pepper and mix well. Stuff salmon with this mixture.

Place fish on foil and garnish with overlapping slices of lemon. Wrap securely in 2 layers of foil. Bake at 350 degrees F for approximately 1 hour, or bake over open fire for 15 to 20 minutes per side.

Serves 6 to 8.

— Carol Swann Jacob
Port McNeill, British Columbia

BABINE RIVER SALMON ROYAL

THE STUFFING AND SAUCE FOR THIS SALMON ARE DELICATE ENOUGH TO ALLOW THE FULL flavour of the fish to be appreciated. The salmon can be barbecued rather than baked for a slightly different flavour.

3-4 lbs. filleted salmon, char or rainbow trout
Salt
¼ cup butter
2 cups soft bread crumbs
¾ tsp. salt
½ tsp. pepper
1 Tbsp. finely chopped parsley
1½ Tbsp. lemon juice
1 cup drained baby clams
1 tsp. tarragon or dill

Drawn Butter Sauce
3 Tbsp. butter
3 Tbsp. flour
1½ cups boiling water
¼ cup butter, cut into ½-inch cubes
½ tsp. salt
1 Tbsp. lemon juice
1 Tbsp. parsley
Lemon wedges

Sprinkle fillets with salt. Melt butter and combine with bread crumbs, salt, pepper, parsley, lemon juice, clams and dill. Lay one fillet, skin side down, on large piece of foil and shape foil up sides of fish. Pile stuffing evenly over fish and top with the other fillet. Bring foil up to overlap edges so that no open flesh is showing, only skin. Place on baking sheet and bake at 450 degrees F for 10 minutes per stuffed inch.

To make sauce, melt 3 Tbsp. butter over low heat and stir in flour to make thick roux. Gradually add boiling water, and stir constantly until smooth. Add the chopped butter gradually, stirring well after each addition. Season with salt and add lemon juice and parsley. Place on platter garnished with parsley and lemon wedges and serve with sauce.

Serves 6 to 8.

— Lori Messer
Topley Landing, British Columbia

SUPER SALMON STUFFING

2 ⅔ cups cooked rice
½ tsp. salt
½ tsp. pepper
½ tsp. sage
½ tsp. thyme
1½ cups minced onion

2 cups chopped celery
½ cup butter
10 lb. salmon
2 cups chopped stuffed olives
Mayonnaise
4 lemon slices

Combine rice, salt, pepper, sage and thyme.

Sauté onion and celery in butter and add to rice mixture. Stir in olives, then spoon stuffing into salmon cavity without packing tightly. Extra stuffing can be baked in a casserole dish. Stitch up the opening.

Spread salmon with a generous amount of mayonnaise, place lemon slices on top and wrap loosely in foil.

Bake at 425 degrees F for 10 minutes per inch of thickness (including stuffing).

Serves 8.

— Penny Everingham
Burford, Ontario

BAKED TROUT WITH WALNUT STUFFING

1 onion, finely chopped
¼ cup chopped walnuts
¼ cup finely chopped green pepper
¼ cup butter
3 slices whole wheat bread, cubed

1 tomato, skinned & chopped
1 tsp. fresh basil, crushed
3-4 lb. lake trout, cleaned & head
   removed

Sauté onion, walnuts and green pepper in butter until onion is translucent. Add to bread and toss lightly until well coated. Add tomato and basil and toss again.

Rub cavity of fish with salt, stuff with dressing and sew cavity loosely closed. Place on rack in shallow pan and cover loosely with foil.

Bake at 350 degrees F for 30 to 35 minutes, turning once after 15 minutes.

Serves 4.

— Ann Jeffries
La Ronge, Saskatchewan

HERBED BAKED TROUT

⅓ cup butter
½ lb. mushrooms, chopped
2 cloves garlic, crushed
¼ cup chopped fresh herbs (parsley, chives,
   tarragon, chervil, etc.)

1 Tbsp. lemon juice
Salt & pepper
4 trout, cleaned

Melt half the butter in a small pan and sauté mushrooms and garlic. Add half the herb mixture, lemon juice, salt and pepper. Stuff the trout with this mixture. Butter pieces of foil, then lay one trout on each. Sprinkle with remaining herb mixture, then dot with remaining butter. Season with salt and pepper and wrap up foil. Lay in baking dish and bake at 350 degrees F for 30 to 40 minutes. Fish should be firm and should flake easily with a fork.

Serves 4.

— Katherine Dunster
Golden, British Columbia

Stuffed Trout, page 193

Back row, *Caper Sauce, page 222*, **left**; *Sauce Verte, page 225*, **right**. **Centre**, *Seafood Sauce, page 222*. **Middle row**, *Escoffier Sauce, page 225*, **left**; *Tartar Sauce, page 223*, **right**. **Front**, *Cucumber Dill Sauce, page 222*

Counterclockwise from top right, *Sui Muy, page 88; Tempura, page 219; Sushi, page 170*

Broiled Salmon Steaks with Herbed Garlic Butter, page 216

Curried Shrimp, Grape & Cashew Salad, page 132

Sole Mousse, page 95

Back row, left to right, *Pickled Herring, page 139; Marinated Mussels, page 134; Marinated Shrimp & Mushrooms, page 94; Pickled Fish, page 101.* **In crocks, back to front**, *Kipper Pâté, page 100; Tapenade, page 96; Salmon Butter, page 99*

Left to right, *Pissaladière Niçoise, page 86; Octopus Salad, page 136; Shrimp Stuffed Cherry Tomatoes, page 133*

FENNEL-RICE STUFFING FOR FISH

1 large onion, chopped
½ cup diced celery
2 cloves garlic, chopped
¼ cup chopped parsley
¼-½ tsp. tarragon

¼-½ tsp. fennel
Salt & pepper
Tabasco sauce
1½ cups cooked rice
1 lemon, thinly sliced

Sauté onion, celery, garlic and seasonings until onion is translucent. Combine with rice, adjusting seasonings if necessary.

Stuff fish and place lemon slices in cavity on top of stuffing.

Makes 2¼ cups of stuffing.

— Wendy Vine
Ganges, British Columbia

STUFFED TROUT

2 cups cooked rice
1 cup hot mango chutney
8 trout, cleaned
½ cup melted butter

Combine rice and chutney and stuff trout. Drizzle with melted butter.

Bake at 375 degrees F for 30 minutes or until fish flakes easily with a fork.

Serves 8.

— Jo & Jerry Huigh
Saskatoon, Saskatchewan

UNCLE CHRIS'S BAKED BASS

8-10 bass, skinned & filleted

Dressing
¼ cup finely chopped ham
1 small onion, finely chopped
¼ green pepper, finely chopped
1 stalk celery, finely chopped
1 slice bacon, finely chopped
Worcestershire sauce
1 tsp. oil
1 Tbsp. lemon juice
2 Tbsp. grated Romano cheese
Thyme
½ tsp. oregano

Topping
⅛ cup bread crumbs

½ tsp. Worcestershire sauce
4-6 strips bacon
2 carrots, sliced
2 stalks celery, sliced
¾ green pepper, sliced
4 onions, quartered
1 cup stewed tomatoes
Water

Sauce
¾ cup sliced mushrooms
¼ cup butter
¼ cup flour
1 cup milk

Arrange half the fillets on bottom of lightly greased shallow baking dish. Combine dressing ingredients in bowl, mixing well. Spread over fillets and top with remaining fish.

For topping, coat fish with Worcestershire sauce and sprinkle with bread crumbs. Lay strips of bacon over fish to cover. Arrange carrots, celery, green pepper and onion around fillets. Top with stewed tomatoes and add ½ cup water. Bake at 350 degrees F.

Meanwhile, sauté mushrooms in butter. Reduce heat and add flour, stirring constantly. Slowly add milk and cook, stirring, until it thickens. Pour over fish after it has cooked for 35 minutes. Bake for 10 more minutes.

Serves 4.

— George Londos
Rosemont, Ontario

STUFFED FILLET ROLLS

SERVED ON A BED OF STEAMED GREENS, THESE THIN FILLETS STUFFED WITH A VEGETABLE OR mushroom mixture make an attractive dish.

1 lb. fish fillets (sole, perch or pickerel)
Salt & pepper
Butter

Vegetable Filling
2 Tbsp. chopped onion
½ cup chopped cucumber
½ cup chopped tomato
2 tsp. lemon juice
2 Tbsp. melted butter

Mushroom Filling
1 Tbsp. butter
2 Tbsp. chopped onion
1 cup chopped mushrooms
⅛ tsp. tarragon

Skin fish, if necessary, and cut into slices 6 inches by 2 inches. Butter a muffin tin or 8 to 10 custard cups, then line each with a piece of fish. Season lightly with salt and pepper.

To make vegetable filling, combine all ingredients and mix well.

For mushroom filling, melt butter, add remaining ingredients, then cook over low heat until softened. Drain.

Place 2 Tbsp. of either filling in centre of each fillet. Bake at 450 degrees for 15 minutes.

Serves 4

— *Nan Millette*
Corunna, Ontario

SCAMPI WITH GARLIC BUTTER

WHEN SERVING THIS DISH, BE SURE TO PROVIDE LOTS OF GOOD BREAD TO DUNK IN THE garlic butter.

2 lbs. large raw shrimp
½ cup butter
1 tsp. salt
6 cloves garlic, crushed

¼ cup chopped parsley
2 tsp. grated lemon peel
2 Tbsp. lemon juice
6 lemon wedges

Remove shells from shrimp, except for tail section. Devein, rinse and drain.

Melt butter in 9" x 13" baking dish in 400 degree F oven. Add salt, garlic and 1 Tbsp. parsley and mix well. Arrange shrimp in single layer in this dish and bake, uncovered, for about 5 minutes. Turn shrimp, sprinkle with lemon peel, lemon juice and remaining parsley. Bake for 8 to 10 minutes or until just tender.

Arrange shrimp on warmed platter and pour garlic butter over them. Serve with lemon wedges.

Serves 6 to 8.

— *Anna Sarraino*
Weston, Ontario

SMUDDER FISH

3-lb. grouper
4-6 potatoes, sliced ½-inch thick
3 carrots, chopped
2 stalks celery, chopped
½ green pepper, chopped

1 stalk broccoli, broken into florets
¼ lb. mushrooms, sliced
1 zucchini, sliced
Lime slices
Butter

Butter a sheet of aluminum foil large enough to place the fish on. Place sliced potatoes on foil. Combine remaining vegetables.

Stuff fish with half the vegetable mixture, and place on top of potatoes. Score top of fish, and place half a lime slice in each cut. Cover with remaining vegetable mixture and dot with butter. Cover with foil and seal loosely.

Barbecue or bake at 350 degrees F for 1 to 1½ hours or until fish flakes and vegetables are tender.

Serves 4.

— *Joan Cox*
Healey Lake, Ontario

STUFFED HADDOCK

1 cup sliced celery
1 small onion, chopped
1½ cups sliced mushrooms
⅓ cup butter
1 cup white rice
¼ tsp. thyme
2 tsp. grated lemon rind

¼ cup lemon juice
2 cups chicken stock
½ cup cooked shrimp
3-5-lb. haddock
1 small grapefruit, thinly sliced
1½ tsp. salt
½ tsp. white pepper

Sauté celery, onion and mushrooms in butter until limp. Add rice, stir until well coated with butter and cook until beginning to turn golden. Add thyme, lemon rind, lemon juice and enough chicken stock to cover rice. Bring to a boil, reduce heat, cover and simmer until liquid has been absorbed, stirring once or twice. Add more stock and continue to cook until rice is tender and fluffy. Remove from heat and stir in shrimp. Let stand for about 5 minutes.

Fill haddock with stuffing and close with skewers. Grease a large piece of aluminum foil, place grapefruit slices on both sides of fish, season with salt and pepper and wrap in foil. Bake at 375 degrees F for approximately 1 hour, turning once.

Serves 6 to 8.

— *Carmen Cockburn*
Halifax, Nova Scotia

STUFFED CHAR WITH GREEN SAUCE

2 lemons, sliced
1 onion, sliced
2 cups parsley
6-lb. Arctic char, cleaned

Green Sauce
1 cup mayonnaise

2 Tbsp. finely chopped spinach
2 Tbsp. finely chopped chives
2 Tbsp. finely chopped parsley
½ Tbsp. tarragon
1 tsp. lemon juice

Place a layer of lemon slices in fish cavity, then layer of onions and one of parsley. Top with remaining lemon slices. Wrap fish tightly in aluminum foil and bake for 10 minutes per inch of thickness, adding 5 minutes for the stuffing, at 350 degrees F or until fish flakes easily.

Meanwhile, prepare Green Sauce by combining all ingredients and mixing well. Refrigerate until ready to use.

When fish is cooked, place on serving platter and serve with sauce.

Serves 10 to 12.

— *Barbara Webb*
Winnipeg, Manitoba

DANDELION STUFFED TROUT

6 Tbsp. butter
2 shallots, finely diced
½ cup sliced mushrooms
6 oz. young dandelion leaves
  (spinach may be substituted)
Parsley

Tarragon
Salt & pepper
2 trout, cleaned
2 Tbsp. orange juice
1 tsp. lemon juice
Cornstarch

Melt 3 Tbsp. butter in skillet, add shallots, mushrooms, dandelion leaves and herbs and sauté quickly until most of the moisture has evaporated.

Stuff fish with mixture. Melt remaining butter and pan-fry trout for 10 minutes on each side or until flaky. Transfer to warm serving platter.

Pour fruit juices into skillet, stir in cornstarch to thicken and cook until medium-thick. Pour over trout and serve.

Serves 2.

— Charlene Skidmore
Medicine Hat, Alberta

TAMARI BAKED FISH

½ cup tamari sauce
½ cup water
2 Tbsp. grated ginger
½ cup minced scallions
2 cloves garlic, crushed

2 tsp. oil
2 tsp. cider vinegar
2 tsp. sugar
2 lbs. fish fillets

Combine all ingredients except fish and whisk together. Let stand for 15 minutes. Marinate fish for 2 to 3 hours, then bake at 350 degrees F for 10 minutes per inch of thickness.

Serves 4.

— Veronica Clarke-Hanik
Toronto, Ontario

CRAB STUFFED SHELLS WITH MORNAY SAUCE

7-oz. can crabmeat
3 Tbsp. minced celery
¼ tsp. salt
⅛ tsp. pepper
¼ cup mayonnaise
¼ tsp. lemon juice
12 jumbo pasta shells,
  cooked & drained

Sauce
3 Tbsp. butter
3 Tbsp. flour
1½ cups milk
1 cup grated Swiss cheese
2 Tbsp. Parmesan cheese
¼ tsp. salt
Pepper

Combine crabmeat, celery, salt, pepper, mayonnaise and lemon juice. Stuff cooked shells with this and place in greased baking dish.

To make sauce, melt butter, add flour and stir. Slowly whisk in milk. Bring to a gentle boil, stirring constantly, and cook for 2 minutes. Remove from heat, add ⅔ cup Swiss cheese and Parmesan cheese. Add salt. Return to medium heat and cook, stirring, until smooth. Pour over stuffed shells and sprinkle with remaining Swiss cheese.

Bake at 350 degrees F for 20 to 25 minutes.

Serves 3 to 4.

— Donna Parker
Pictou, Nova Scotia

Casseroles

Un-dish-cover the fish, or
dishcover the riddle.

**– Through the Looking Glass
Lewis Carroll**

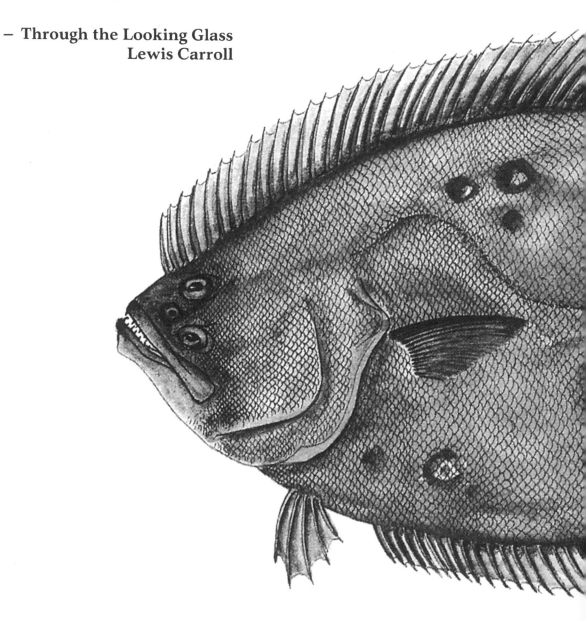

SEAFOOD IN FILO PASTRY

2 Tbsp. butter
½ cup thinly sliced celery
½ cup chopped onion
1 cup sliced mushrooms
4 Tbsp. flour
1 tsp. salt
1½ cups milk
½ cup white wine

2 Tbsp. lemon juice
¼ cup grated Parmesan cheese
½ lb. cooked shrimp
½ lb. cooked sole
1 lb. cooked salmon
8 sheets filo pastry
¾ cup melted butter

Melt butter in large, heavy saucepan. Add celery and onion and cook until tender. Add mushrooms and continue cooking. Stir in flour and salt. Add milk slowly, stirring constantly, and cook until thickened. Stir in wine, lemon juice and cheese. Cook until thickened, stirring constantly. Remove from heat and add seafood.

Grease 9″ x 13″ baking dish. Brush each sheet of pastry with melted butter and layer in dish. When all 8 sheets are buttered and in dish, spoon a row of filling down the middle of pastry.

Fold both sides in, so they overlap. Flip gently so seam is facing down. Tuck ends under and brush top with remaining butter.

Bake at 375 degrees F for 45 minutes or until crisp and golden brown.

Serves 8.

— Susan Gillespie
Comox, British Columbia

GREEK PASTRY STUFFED WITH FISH & SPINACH

THIS RECIPE TAKES A BIT OF TIME TO PREPARE, BUT THE RESULTING DISH IS WELL WORTH THE effort. Filo pastry can be found in most Italian and Greek specialty stores. It can be stored in the freezer for several months if necessary.

Filling
1½ lbs. spinach, washed & coarsely
   chopped
Butter
1 bunch green onions, sliced
¾ lb. Boston bluefish, chopped
½ green pepper, minced
4 eggs, lightly beaten
¼ cup lemon juice
Salt & pepper
1½ tsp. dill weed
1 tsp. garlic powder

Pastry
2 cups butter
⅓ cup lemon juice
1 Tbsp. garlic powder
1 lb. filo pastry

To make filling, sauté spinach in butter until limp. Combine with remaining ingredients in bowl and set aside.

For dough, combine butter, lemon juice and garlic powder in saucepan. Cook over low heat until butter is melted. Unwrap filo dough on large working area. Fold one sheet lengthwise in thirds and brush with butter mixture. Fold and butter a second sheet similarly. Place strips end to end, overlapping by ½ inch. Place 2 Tbsp. filling near one end and fold pastry into triangle shape, folding over and over until all dough is used. Place on greased cookie sheet. Repeat with remaining dough and filling. Drizzle with remaining butter mixture and bake at 350 degrees F for 30 minutes, or until golden brown and puffed.

Makes 12 triangles.

— Titia Posthuma
Maberly, Ontario

SEAFOOD VEGETABLE TREASURES

½ lb. scallops, diced if large
½ lb. shrimp
Juice of 1 lemon
½ cup butter
2 cups sliced mushrooms
1 cup chopped celery
¾ cup chopped onion
¾ cup chopped green pepper

¼ cup flour
1½ cups milk
1 cup grated Swiss cheese
Salt & pepper
1 cup soft bread crumbs
½ cup chopped cashews or almonds
2 Tbsp. melted butter

Combine scallops and shrimp and sprinkle lemon juice over them. Toss and set aside.

Melt ¼ cup butter and cook mushrooms, celery, onion and green pepper until tender — about 5 minutes. Set aside.

Melt remaining butter in large saucepan and blend in flour. Cook for 1 minute, then gradually add milk and cook until thickened, stirring constantly. Remove from heat. Stir in cheese and salt and pepper. Gently fold in vegetables and seafood, then spoon into 6 individual au gratin dishes.

Combine bread crumbs, nuts and melted butter and sprinkle on top. Bake at 350 degrees F for 25 to 30 minutes or until hot and bubbly.

Serves 6.

— *Heather Yates*
North Vancouver, British Columbia

SALMON TETRAZZINI

TETRAZZINI IS MORE TRADITIONALLY MADE WITH TURKEY OR CHICKEN, BUT IT IS EQUALLY delicious when salmon or tuna is used.

1 cup raw spaghetti noodles
4 Tbsp. butter
1 onion, chopped
1 clove garlic, crushed
2 Tbsp. flour
Salt & pepper
Dill weed
1 tsp. thyme

4 Tbsp. dry sherry
2-3 cups light cream
2 cups grated Swiss cheese
2 cups sliced mushrooms
1 cup sliced almonds
16-oz. can salmon, drained & flaked
⅓ cup grated Parmesan cheese

Cook noodles until tender, drain, rinse well with cold water and set aside.

Melt 2 Tbsp. butter over high heat. Sauté onion and garlic until transparent, then stir in flour and cook over medium heat for 2 minutes. Add salt, pepper, dill, thyme and sherry. Slowly stir in cream and cook, stirring, until thickened. Add Swiss cheese and cook over low heat until cheese is melted.

Melt remaining 2 Tbsp. butter in another skillet and sauté mushrooms and almonds for 5 minutes.

Combine noodles, salmon, cheese sauce and mushroom mixture and place in a greased casserole dish. Top with Parmesan cheese and bake at 350 degrees F for 30 minutes.

Serves 4 to 6.

PUFFED SALMON CREPES

Crêpes

¾ cup flour
¼ tsp. salt
2 eggs
½ cup milk
½ cup water
1 Tbsp. melted butter

Filling

4 Tbsp. butter
1 onion, diced
2 stalks celery, chopped
4 Tbsp. flour
16½-oz. can salmon, drained with
  liquid reserved
Milk to make 1¾ cups when combined
  with salmon liquid

1 cup grated Cheddar cheese
Pepper
Tarragon
Dill
Lemon juice

Custard

2 eggs
½ cup sour cream
¾ cup milk
Salt & pepper
Curry powder

Topping

⅓ cup sour cream
Dill

To make crêpes, place flour and salt in bowl and mix to combine. Make a well in it and add eggs and milk. Beat with a fork while adding water, until all the flour has come away from the sides of the bowl. If batter is too thick, add another tablespoon of water. Refrigerate for a couple of hours.

For filling, melt butter and sauté onion and celery until onion is translucent but celery is still crisp. Add flour and stir. Add salmon juice and milk gradually, stirring well. Cook over medium heat until thickened. Add cheese and continue to cook, stirring, until thickened. Add salmon and seasonings and remove from heat.

Melt 1 Tbsp. butter in small, heavy skillet and cook crêpes one at a time by gently pouring in a few tablespoons of batter and swirling it around to cover bottom of skillet. When browned on one side, flip and cook briefly on the other. Stack crêpes until all are cooked.

Divide filling among crêpes, place in centre of each crêpe, then fold ends over middle to enclose filling. Place crêpes in single layer in greased baking dish.

Combine custard ingredients and mix well. Pour over crêpes. Bake at 350 degrees F for 45 to 50 minutes or until puffed. Spread with sour cream and dill and return to oven for another 10 minutes.

Serves 4.

— Rosande Bellaar-Spruyt
Rupert, Quebec

SALMON & BROCCOLI

1 bunch broccoli, coarsely chopped
1 Tbsp. lemon juice
3 Tbsp. butter
3 Tbsp. flour
3 cups milk
½ cup grated Parmesan cheese

½ tsp. cayenne
⅛ tsp. nutmeg
1 tsp. dry mustard
16-oz. can salmon
4 Tbsp. pine nuts or sunflower seeds

Place broccoli in bottom of shallow casserole dish and sprinkle with lemon juice.

In saucepan, melt butter and add flour, stirring with a whisk. Gradually stir in milk and cook over low heat, stirring constantly, until thickened.

Add Parmesan cheese, cayenne, nutmeg and mustard and cook for 1 minute. Add salmon with its juice. Pour over broccoli, sprinkle with pine nuts or sunflower seeds and bake at 400 degrees F for 15 to 20 minutes.

Serves 4.

— Cheryl Veitch
Bella Coola, British Columbia

SEAFOOD LASAGNE

18 lasagne noodles
1 lb. spinach, briefly cooked & chopped
4 eggs, lightly beaten
1 lb. ricotta cheese
Salt & pepper
Nutmeg
6 Tbsp. butter
1 onion, chopped

1 clove garlic, crushed
1 Tbsp. chopped dill
6 Tbsp. flour
2 Tbsp. sherry
3 cups cream
1 cup grated Swiss cheese
6-oz. can crabmeat
½ cup grated Parmesan cheese

Cook noodles until tender, drain and rinse well under cold water. Set aside.

Combine spinach, eggs, ricotta cheese, salt, pepper and nutmeg and mix well.

Melt butter and sauté onion and garlic until limp. Add dill, flour and salt and pepper and cook over medium heat for 2 minutes. Stir in sherry and cream and cook, stirring, until thickened. Add Swiss cheese and crab and heat through.

Place half the noodles in the bottom of a greased 9″ x 13″ casserole dish. Spread half the spinach mixture over this, then half the cheese sauce. Repeat. Top with Parmesan cheese and bake at 350 degrees F for 30 minutes.

Serves 6.

— *Shirley Lockhart*
St. Catharines, Ontario

SEASIDE MANICOTTI

6 manicotti shells
10 oz. spinach
½ cup chopped onion
1 clove garlic, crushed
2 Tbsp. butter
3 Tbsp. flour
2 cups milk

1 cup Swiss cheese
¼ cup grated Parmesan cheese
2 Tbsp. butter, melted
½ tsp. salt
1 lb. perch fillets, cooked & flaked
Ground nutmeg

Cook manicotti shells and drain. Cook spinach and drain.

Meanwhile, prepare cheese sauce. Cook onion and garlic in 2 Tbsp. butter until tender but not brown. Blend in flour. Add milk all at once. Cook and stir until thick and bubbly. Stir in Swiss cheese and cook until melted.

Combine ½ cup of sauce with the spinach, Parmesan cheese, 2 Tbsp. melted butter and salt. Fold in flaked fish. Stuff manicotti shells with this mixture.

Pour half of remaining sauce into baking dish. Put manicotti on top and pour remaining sauce over.

Cover and bake at 350 degrees F for 30 to 35 minutes. Sprinkle nutmeg over top before serving.

Serves 6.

— *Mary Ann Vanner*
Kingston, Ontario

PENNE WITH CRAB & SHRIMP SAUCE

12 oz. penne
8 oz. shrimp
8 oz. crab
¼ cup butter
1 tsp. curry powder
¼ cup flour

¼ tsp. salt
¼ tsp. pepper
2 cups milk
½ cup grated mozzarella cheese
Parmesan cheese

Cook and drain penne. Sauté shrimp and crab in butter and curry for 3 to 4 minutes. Blend in flour, salt and pepper. Gradually stir in milk and mozzarella cheese, and cook until thick.

Pour sauce over penne, stir, and place in greased casserole dish. Sprinkle with Parmesan cheese. Bake at 350 degrees F until bubbly hot, then broil to brown cheese.

Serves 6.

— Carrol Chura
Victoria, British Columbia

CHEESY FISH WITH SPINACH NOODLES

1 cup water
½ tsp. salt
2 lbs. fish fillets
2 onions, thinly sliced
4 stalks celery, chopped
1 cup sliced mushrooms
6 Tbsp. butter

3 Tbsp. flour
2½ cups light cream
Salt & pepper
1 cup grated sharp Cheddar cheese
1 lb. spinach fettuccine
Butter

Bring salted water to a boil, add fish, and simmer for 10 minutes, or until fish is cooked. In heavy skillet, sauté onions, celery and mushrooms in 3 Tbsp. butter until limp. Remove and set aside. Add remaining butter to pan. When melted, stir in flour and cook for 2 minutes. Add cream slowly and cook until thick. Season to taste. Arrange fish in greased casserole dish, top with vegetables, and pour sauce over all. Sprinkle with grated cheese.

Bake at 375 degrees F for 15 minutes or until hot and bubbly.

Meanwhile, cook noodles until just tender, drain, rinse, and toss with butter.

Serve noodles topped with fish.

Serves 6 to 8.

— Leslie Hawkins
Thunder Bay, Ontario

SUPER SEAFOOD CASSEROLE

2 cups chopped onions
3 cups chopped celery
2 cloves garlic, crushed
3 Tbsp. butter
½ cup butter
¾ cup flour
¾ tsp. salt

¼ tsp. pepper
4½ cups milk
1½ cups grated Cheddar cheese
¾ lb. lobster
½ lb. crab
¾ lb. shrimp
1 lb. scallops

Sauté onions, celery and garlic in 3 Tbsp. butter.

Melt ½ cup butter and stir in flour, salt and pepper. Cook, stirring, over medium heat for 2 minutes. Slowly add milk and cook, stirring, until thickened. Stir in cheese and cook until it melts. Add lobster, crab, shrimp, scallops and sautéed vegetables and mix well. Place in a greased casserole dish.

Bake at 350 degrees F for 30 minutes or until bubbly.

Serves 8.

— Mary Lou Garlick
Pine Point, Northwest Territories

SCALLOPS IN WINE

2 lbs. scallops
2 cups white wine
¼ cup butter
4 shallots, finely chopped
24 mushroom caps, finely sliced

2 Tbsp. parsley
2 Tbsp. flour
2-4 Tbsp. whipping cream
½-1 cup bread crumbs
Butter

Wash scallops and simmer in wine for 5 minutes. Drain and reserve liquid.

Melt butter and sauté shallots, mushroom caps and parsley. Stir in flour. Add reserved liquid and whipping cream and cook until slightly thickened. Stir in scallops and place in greased, shallow casserole dish. Top with bread crumbs and dot with butter. Broil until golden brown.

Serves 4.

— *Kathy Payette*
Kitchener, Ontario

CREAMY SCALLOP SHELLS

1 lb. bay scallops
6 Tbsp. butter
½ cup chopped scallions
¼ lb. mushrooms, sliced
1 Tbsp. flour
½ cup white wine
½ cup whipping cream

6 Tbsp. grated Parmesan cheese
3 egg yolks, beaten
1 tsp. lemon juice
18 giant pasta shells
2 Tbsp. butter, melted
⅓ cup fine dry bread crumbs

Rinse scallops and dry well. Melt 4 Tbsp. butter in skillet over medium heat. Sauté scallions and mushrooms, then stir in flour and cook, stirring, until bubbly. Pour in wine and cream and cook, stirring, until thick. Add scallops and 3 Tbsp. Parmesan cheese. Bring to a boil, stir, then remove from heat.

Beat some of the hot liquid into the egg yolks, then stir egg mixture into hot scallop mixture. Return to low heat and cook, stirring constantly, until thick. Do not allow to boil. Stir in lemon juice.

Cook pasta shells in boiling water, then rinse with cold water. Brush outside of each shell with melted butter, then fill with about 2 Tbsp. scallop mixture. Place in greased casserole dish.

Melt remaining 2 Tbsp. butter, mix with bread crumbs and remaining 3 Tbsp. cheese and sprinkle over shells as evenly as possible. Bake, covered, at 350 degrees F for 30 minutes or until hot and bubbly.

Serves 4.

— *Elizabeth Otto & Susan Gutmaker*
Denver, Colorado

SHRIMP VIENNESE

6 large mushrooms, diced
½ onion, finely chopped
¼ cup butter
1 Tbsp. flour
1 Tbsp. chopped dill
½ cup chicken stock

½ cup light cream
Juice of ½ lemon
Salt & pepper
½ tsp. paprika
1 lb. shrimp, cooked & peeled
2 cups cooked rice

Cook mushrooms and onion in butter until onions are translucent. Add flour and dill, mix well, then add stock and cream slowly. Bring to a boil, then add lemon juice, salt, pepper and paprika. Simmer until barely thickened, then add shrimp.

Place rice in bottom of a greased casserole dish and pour sauce over top. Bake at 325 degrees F for 15 minutes.

Serves 4.

— *Anne Ulmer*
Cannon Falls, Minnesota

SHRIMP PILAU

8 slices bacon, diced
2 cups finely chopped onion
2 cups rice
3 cups chicken stock
2 cups chopped tomatoes
2 tsp. Worcestershire sauce
1 tsp. mace
½ tsp. cayenne
1 tsp. salt
2 lbs. shrimp
2 Tbsp. chopped parsley

In a heavy 3-quart casserole dish, fry bacon until crisp. Drain on paper towelling and set aside. Reserve 3 Tbsp. bacon fat and cook onion in this until soft. Add rice and cook, stirring, until rice glistens. Mix in stock, tomatoes, Worcestershire sauce and seasonings. Bring to a boil over high heat.

Cover casserole tightly and bake at 350 degrees F for 30 minutes. Add shrimp and bacon, toss gently, recover and bake for 10 minutes longer or until the liquid in the pan has been absorbed. Remove from oven and set aside for 10 minutes. Fluff with a fork, sprinkle with parsley and serve.

Serves 6.

— *Holly Andrews*
Puslinch, Ontario

SHRIMP & WILD RICE CASSEROLE

1½ cups mixed wild & basmati rice
1 onion, chopped
1 lb. mushrooms, sliced
¼ cup lemon juice
2 Tbsp. butter
2 Tbsp. flour
1¼ cups chicken stock
½ cup white wine
½ tsp. salt
¼ tsp. garlic powder
½ tsp. tarragon
3 Tbsp. Parmesan cheese
2 lbs. cooked shrimp

Cook rice until tender in 3 cups boiling water. Sauté onion and mushrooms in oil until onion is translucent, then sprinkle with lemon juice and set aside.

Melt butter in heavy pot. Stir in flour and make a paste, then add chicken stock and wine. Cook, stirring, until thickened. Add salt, garlic powder, tarragon and cheese and stir well. Mix three-quarters of the sauce with the vegetables, then add shrimp and rice. Place in greased casserole dish and pour remaining sauce over top.

Bake at 350 degrees F for 30 minutes.

Serves 6.

— *Leslie Hawkins*
Thunder Bay, Ontario

FILLET OF SOLE FLORENTINE

1 lb. spinach
¼ tsp. sugar
2 Tbsp. butter
2 Tbsp. flour
1 cup milk
Nutmeg
½ cup thinly sliced mushrooms
½ cup grated Cheddar or Swiss cheese
2 Tbsp. chopped parsley
Salt & pepper
1 lb. sole fillets

Wash spinach and pack into a saucepan. Sprinkle with sugar, cover and cook over medium heat for 3 to 4 minutes. Lift lid, turn spinach and cook for an additional 2 minutes. Drain and spread on the bottom of a buttered 1½-quart casserole dish.

Melt butter, stir in flour and cook over low heat for 1 minute. Add milk and stir to blend. Cook until slightly thickened, then add nutmeg, mushrooms, cheese, parsley, salt and pepper.

Spread fillets over spinach, then pour sauce over fish. Bake at 350 degrees F for 30 minutes.

Serves 4.

— *Joann Alho*
Brantford, Ontario

PASTEL DE PESCADO

3 Tbsp. olive oil
½ cup ground almonds
2 cloves garlic, minced
4 onions, chopped
1 bay leaf
2 tsp. salt
1 tsp. pepper
5 tomatoes, peeled & chopped
1½ lbs. sole or other white fish fillets
3 cups mashed potatoes, seasoned with
   salt & pepper

Heat oil in saucepan, add almonds and sauté for 5 minutes. Remove almonds and sauté garlic and onion until softened, adding more oil if necessary. Add bay leaf, salt, pepper and tomatoes, then cook over low heat for 10 minutes, stirring occasionally.

Grind one piece of fish and cut the rest into 2- to 3-inch pieces. Remove and reserve one-third of tomato mixture. To the remaining two-thirds, add the almonds and the ground fish. Cook this mixture over low heat for 10 minutes, stirring to prevent sticking.

Butter a 9″ x 9″ casserole dish. Line bottom and sides with mashed potato, reserving enough to cover top of casserole. Alternate layers of fish and tomato mixture, then cover with reserved mashed potato. Bake at 425 degrees F for 30 minutes. Just before serving, heat reserved tomato mixture to pass as sauce.

Serves 6.

— *Heather Quiney*
Victoria, British Columbia

FISH FILLETS WITH CIDER

1 cup green beans or sliced carrots, cooked
1 tsp. salt
Pepper
Thyme
2 lbs. haddock fillets
½ cup sliced mushrooms
¼ cup chopped green onions
2 Tbsp. chopped parsley
2 Tbsp. bread crumbs
2 Tbsp. grated Cheddar cheese
2 Tbsp. melted butter
1 cup cider
2 Tbsp. lemon juice

Place beans or carrots in bottom of casserole dish. Sprinkle with half the seasonings. Cover with fish, mushrooms, onions, parsley and the rest of the seasonings. Top with bread crumbs, cheese and butter. Combine cider and lemon juice and pour over all. Bake at 425 degrees F for 20 to 25 minutes, or until fish is cooked and top browned.

Serves 8.

— *Winifred Czerny*
Pointe Claire, Quebec

COMPANY FISH CASSEROLE

2 cups flaked cooked fish
1 cup shrimp
2 cups white sauce
2 hard-cooked eggs, sliced
½ cup sautéed mushrooms
4 green onions, chopped
½ cup diced green & red pepper
¼ cup minced parsley
Meringue
2 egg whites, beaten until stiff
½ cup grated cheese

Combine all casserole ingredients in saucepan and simmer. When hot, place in greased casserole dish.

To make meringue, combine beaten egg whites and cheese and blend well.

Spread meringue evenly over fish mixture and bake at 450 degrees F until meringue is well browned — 15 to 20 minutes.

Serves 4.

— *Dawn Millette*
Smiths Falls, Ontario

FISH AU GRATIN

2 cups milk
½ onion, sliced
Bay leaf
2 Tbsp. parsley
3 Tbsp. butter

3 Tbsp. flour
Salt & pepper
2 cups flaked cooked fish
1 cup fine bread crumbs
¼ cup grated Swiss cheese

Scald milk with onion, bay leaf and parsley. Strain.

Melt butter and stir in flour and salt and pepper. When smooth, slowly stir in scalded milk and cook until thickened.

Arrange fish and white sauce in alternate layers in greased casserole dish. Top with bread crumbs and cheese.

Bake at 350 degrees F for 30 minutes or until browned on top.

Serves 4 to 6.

— *Jane Lewis*
Grand River, Nova Scotia

SASKATCHEWAN SPRING DISH

3 Tbsp. butter
3 Tbsp. flour
Cayenne
1 cup cream
1 Tbsp. Cognac
½ tsp. salt

4 perch, skinned
½ cup water
½ cup white wine
1 cup grated Swiss cheese
12 asparagus tips

Melt butter in heavy saucepan. Add flour and cook over medium heat, stirring, until flour is absorbed. Add cayenne, cream, Cognac and salt and cook for 2 to 3 minutes.

Place perch in casserole dish, add water and wine, cover with buttered wax paper and poach at 350 degrees F for 5 minutes. Remove fish from oven and when cooled enough to handle, remove fish from skeleton. Keep warm.

Place fish and asparagus in 2 au gratin dishes, pour cream sauce over them and sprinkle with grated cheese. Bake at 450 degrees F for 5 minutes, or until cheese is melted and bubbly.

Serves 2.

—*Nancy Russell*
Saskatoon, Saskatchewan

VISSHOTEL MET KAAS

THIS IS A DUTCH RECIPE FOR AN INEXPENSIVE, EASY TO PREPARE, YET ATTRACTIVE AND flavourful dish.

1 cup macaroni
2 lbs. cod fillets
2 Tbsp. lemon juice
Salt & pepper
1 large onion, finely chopped

4 Tbsp. butter
2 cups tomato juice
½ cup chopped parsley
½ lb. Gouda cheese, thinly sliced

Butter a 2-quart casserole dish. Put uncooked macaroni on bottom of dish. Sprinkle fish with lemon juice, salt and pepper. Arrange fish on top of macaroni. Sauté onion in butter until tender, add tomato juice and bring mixture to a boil. Add parsley and cook for about 3 to 4 minutes. Pour mixture over fish and cover with slices of cheese. Cover dish and bake at 400 degrees F for 45 minutes, uncovering for last 15 minutes.

Serves 6 to 8.

— *Heleen van der Linden*
Winnipeg, Manitoba

STUFFED FLOUNDER CREOLE

½ cup chopped onion
¼ cup chopped green pepper
2 cloves garlic, minced
¼ cup chopped celery
3 Tbsp. butter
2 Tbsp. chopped parsley
2 Tbsp. chopped pimento
6 slices bread, soaked in water to cover
½ lb. crabmeat
1 tsp. salt
½ tsp. pepper
2 lbs. flounder or sole fillets

Basting Sauce
½ cup melted butter
¼ cup lemon juice
2 cloves garlic, crushed
¼ cup chopped parsley

Sauté onion, green pepper, garlic and celery in butter until softened. Add parsley and pimento. Squeeze excess water from bread, then add bread to vegetables along with crabmeat, salt and pepper. Cook gently for 10 minutes.

Place half the fillets in a shallow, buttered oven dish. Top with crab mixture, then with remaining fillets. Combine ingredients for basting sauce, pour over fish, and bake at 400 degrees F for 25 to 30 minutes, or until fish flakes easily with a fork.

Serves 8.

— Iris Bates
Midhurst, Ontario

MUSSEL-RICE CASSEROLE

6 dozen mussels (to yield 1 lb. meat)
2 Tbsp. butter
1 large onion, chopped
2 cups sliced mushrooms
1 cup chopped celery
2 Tbsp. flour
1½ cups chicken stock
¼ cup chopped parsley

1 Tbsp. lemon juice
1 tsp. salt
⅛ tsp. pepper
½ cup raisins
4 cups cooked brown rice
1 lemon, sliced
Parsley sprigs

To prepare mussels, scrub the shells in water to remove any debris and then place in a large pot with 2 inches of water. Cover, bring to a boil and steam until shells open. Drain, and remove meat from shells.

Melt butter and sauté onion, mushrooms and celery until tender. Remove from pan and set aside. Stir flour into remaining butter, gradually add stock and cook over medium heat, stirring, until thickened. Add chopped parsley, lemon juice, salt and pepper.

Combine sauce, mussels, raisins and rice in a greased casserole dish. Bake at 375 degrees F for 20 minutes. Garnish with lemon slices and parsley.

Serves 4.

— Heather Quiney
Victoria, British Columbia

CHICKEN HADDIE SUPREME

5 slices bread
14-oz. can chicken haddie
1 cup grated Cheddar cheese
Butter

Salt & pepper
4 eggs, beaten
2¼ cups milk

Grease a 10″ x 10″ pan. Arrange 4 slices of bread in the bottom of pan. Cover with half the fish, then sprinkle with half the cheese. Add remaining fish and remaining cheese.

Butter fifth slice of bread, then cut into four quarters. Arrange on top of casserole and sprinkle with salt and pepper. Combine eggs and milk, then pour over casserole. Bake at 375 degrees F for 45 minutes.

Serves 4.

— Billie Sheffield
North Gower, Ontario

SCALLOP BUBBLY BAKE

½ cup chopped onion
1½ cups chopped celery
1 cup chopped green pepper
1 cup sliced mushrooms
2 Tbsp. butter
1 lb. scallops

¼ cup butter
¼ cup flour
1 tsp. salt
2 cups milk
1 cup buttered bread crumbs
¾ cup grated mozzarella cheese

Sauté vegetables in 2 Tbsp. butter. Cover scallops with cold water, bring to a boil and cook for 1 minute. Drain, place in greased casserole dish and mix with vegetables.

Melt ¼ cup butter and stir in flour and salt. Cook for 1 minute, then slowly stir in milk and cook, stirring, until thickened. Pour over casserole.

Top with buttered bread crumbs and cheese, and bake at 350 degrees F for 30 minutes or until brown and bubbly.

Serves 4.

— Gladys Long
Wolfville, Nova Scotia

FILLETS OF SOLE SIBOUR WITH SHRIMP

16 sole fillets
Salt & pepper
2 stalks celery, finely chopped
1 onion, finely chopped
1 clove garlic, crushed
½ cup finely chopped blanched
    almonds
2 Tbsp. butter
¼ cup chicken stock
1 cup soft bread crumbs
Mace
Nutmeg
Thyme

1 tsp. salt
¼ cup melted butter
¼ cup white wine

Shrimp Sauce
2 Tbsp. butter
2 Tbsp. flour
1 cup milk
1 lb. shrimp
1 tsp. salt
3 Tbsp. sherry

Season fillets with salt and pepper. Sauté celery and onion with garlic and almonds in butter until onion is transparent. Add chicken stock and bread crumbs, and season with mace, nutmeg, thyme and salt. Place filling equally on top of fillets, roll up and secure with toothpicks. Pour melted butter into shallow casserole dish and arrange fillets on top. Sprinkle with white wine, and bake at 350 degrees F for 10 minutes, turn and then bake for another 10 minutes.

To make sauce, melt butter and blend in flour. Add milk slowly. Cook over medium heat, stirring, until thickened. Add shrimp and salt and heat through. When ready to serve, stir in sherry. Pour over sole and serve.

Serves 6 to 8.

— Pauline Longmore
Chilliwack, British Columbia

PAELLA

As in most regional dishes, the ingredients for paella vary from cook to cook. This version combines meat and seafood in a colourful, festive presentation. Other possible ingredients include sausage, octopus, clams and crayfish or lobster. It is traditionally baked over a wood fire, in a shallow, two-handled, hammered-steel dish, but a large frying pan or heavy casserole dish will do just as well.

2 cups fresh peas or green beans
2 lbs. halibut, cut into chunks
1 lb. mussels, scrubbed
1 lb. shrimp, shelled & deveined
½ lb. squid, cleaned & cut into rings
1 tsp. saffron threads
½ cup olive oil
½ lb. ham, cut into chunks

1 whole chicken breast, boned & cut
  into chunks
2 tomatoes, sliced
1 large clove garlic, peeled & sliced
2 Tbsp. sweet paprika
3 cups long-grain rice
2 sweet red peppers, roasted, peeled
  & cut into strips

Cook peas or beans in water until just tender. Drain, saving water. Add water to make 5 cups. Bring to a boil, add fish, mussels, shrimp and squid, and simmer for 5 minutes.

Lift out seafood, and set aside. Add saffron to cooking water and let stand. In the pan in which you plan to present the paella, heat the olive oil. Sauté ham and chicken in oil until just done, and set aside. In same oil, sauté tomatoes and garlic; add paprika and cook gently for a couple of minutes. Sprinkle rice into pan, cover with peas or beans, halibut, shrimp, ham, chicken and squid. Pour water with saffron over top and bring to a boil. Continue boiling while arranging mussels and strips of pepper on top.

Place in a preheated 400 degree F oven for 15 minutes. Remove from oven and cook on top of stove for a minute or so. Serve immediately.

Serves 8.

SOLE WITH CREAMY CRABMEAT SAUCE

2 lbs. sole fillets
4 cups poaching liquid (Court
  Bouillon, fish stock, wine, water

Sauce
4 Tbsp. butter
2 green onions, sliced
½ lb. mushrooms, sliced

6½-oz. can crabmeat, flaked
4 Tbsp. flour
Salt & pepper
Dill
3 cups light cream
½ cup grated Parmesan cheese

Poach sole in liquid until fish flakes easily with a fork — 15 minutes. Remove from poaching liquid and set aside.

To prepare sauce, melt butter and sauté onions and mushrooms for 3 to 5 minutes. Stir in crabmeat. Add flour and cook over medium heat for 1 minute. Add salt and pepper and dill to taste. Gradually add cream, stirring constantly, and cook until sauce thickens. Stir in cheese.

Place sole in ovenproof dish in single layer. Pour sauce over top and bake at 350 degrees F until bubbly and golden brown.

Serves 4.

Miscellaneous

A piece of broiled fish, and of an honeycomb.

– St. Luke 24:42

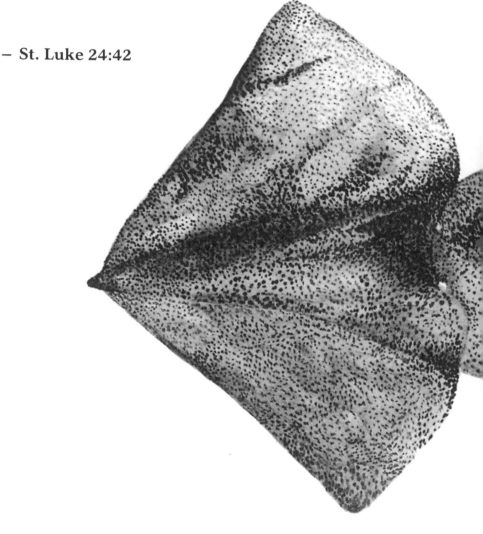

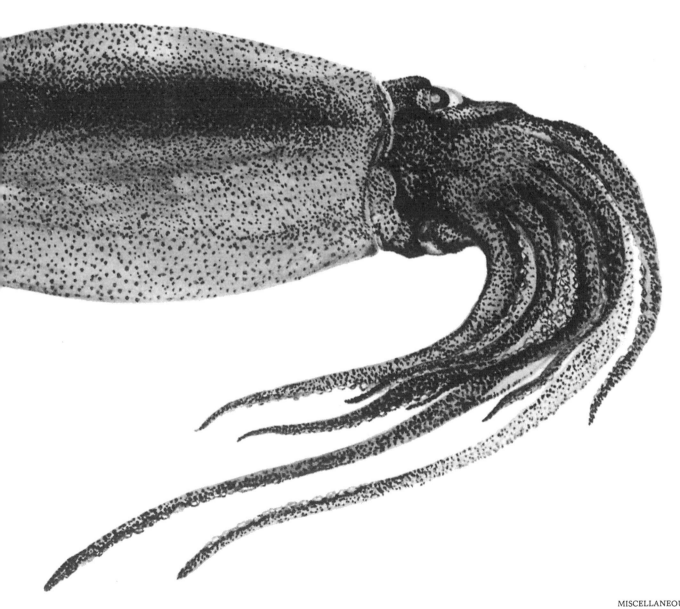

COCONUT BEER SHRIMP WITH MARMALADE SAUCE

6 oz. beer
½ cup flour
1½ tsp. baking powder
½ tsp. salt
½ tsp. white pepper
24 shrimp, peeled & deveined but
   with tails intact

Flour
1 cup shredded coconut
Oil for deep frying

Marmalade Sauce
½ cup creole mustard
½ cup orange marmalade

Combine beer, flour, baking powder, salt and pepper in blender and process until completely smooth. Dust shrimp with flour, shaking off excess, then dip in batter, covering completely. Roll in coconut.

To make marmalade sauce combine mustard and marmalade in small bowl and mix thoroughly.

Deep fry shrimp in oil heated to 375 degrees F until golden brown – 2 to 3 minutes. Drain. Serve immediately with Marmalade Sauce.

Serves 4.

— *L.M. Cyre*
Logan Lake, British Columbia

BAVARIAN SMELTS

2 lbs. fresh smelts, cleaned
1½ cups beer
1 cup flour

Salt & pepper
Oil for frying
Lemon wedges

Place smelts in bowl and pour beer over them. Cover and refrigerate for 1 hour. Heat 1 inch oil in frying pan to 375 degrees F. Drain smelts, reserving beer. Season flour with salt and pepper. Roll each fish in flour, then dip in beer, then once more in flour. Fry until golden brown. Serve with lemon wedges.

Serves 6 to 8.

— *Emilia Williams*
Sable River, Nova Scotia

OYSTER FRITTERS

2 eggs
1 cup flour
½ tsp. salt
Milk to make ½ cup liquid
   including oyster juice
1 tsp. baking powder

2 tsp. melted shortening
18 large fresh oysters, chopped finely
   with juice reserved
1 large onion, finely chopped
Oil for deep frying

Beat eggs for 1 minute. Add flour, salt, milk, baking powder and shortening. Stir in oysters and onion.

Heat oil in deep pan to 375 degrees F. Drop batter by teaspoonfuls into oil and cook for 2 to 3 minutes. Drain well and serve.

Serves 5 to 6.

— *Dianne Vanderberg*
Qualicum Beach, British Columbia

DEEP FRIED SCALLOPS WITH SEAFOOD SAUCE

Sauce
½ cup sugar
½ cup vinegar
Salt
1 cup pineapple juice
⅛ tsp. ground ginger
½ tsp. soya sauce
1 tsp. tomato paste
½ Tbsp. cornstarch dissolved in small
    amount of water

2 cups crushed cracker crumbs
Salt & pepper
Pinch saffron
1 lb. scallops
1 egg, well beaten
Oil for deep frying

To make sauce, heat all ingredients except cornstarch to boiling point. Slowly add cornstarch paste and continue to cook, stirring, for 2 to 3 minutes.

Combine cracker crumbs, salt, pepper and saffron. Moisten scallops in egg, then dredge with crumb mixture. Cook in oil heated to 375 degrees F until golden brown — 3 to 5 minutes — then drain well and serve with sauce.

Serves 4.

— Donna Parker
Pictou, Nova Scotia

P.E.I. FISH FRIED A NEW WAY

1 lb. fish fillets
1 egg, beaten
¼ cup milk
½ cup ground oat flour (blend 1¼ cups quick
    cooking oats for 1 minute or until oats
    are reduced to a powder)
½ cup yellow corn meal

1 tsp. baking powder
1 tsp. paprika
¾ tsp. salt
Large pinch dry mustard
Oil
Lemons

Cut fish into serving-sized pieces. Combine egg and milk and dip fish pieces in mixture.

Combine remaining ingredients except oil and lemons, mixing thoroughly, then coat fish with this.

Heat ½ inch oil, then fry fish quickly, turning once — allow approximately 10 minutes per inch of fish.

Drain on paper towels. Serve with lemon wedges.

Serves 4.

— J.W. Houston
Willowdale, Ontario

GOLDEN FISH DISH

4 cod fillets, ½-inch thick
Oil
12 asparagus spears
½ cup sour cream

1 egg, separated
1 tsp. horseradish
1 Tbsp. chopped parsley

Brush fillets with oil and place in greased baking dish. Broil for 8 minutes or until fish flakes.

Meanwhile, lightly steam asparagus. Place 3 spears on each fillet.

To make topping, combine sour cream, egg yolk, horseradish and parsley. Beat egg white until firm and fold in. Spread over fillets and asparagus and broil for 2 to 3 minutes or until puffy and golden brown.

Serves 2 to 4.

— Isobel Brown
Grantham's Landing, British Columbia

BROILED SALMON STEAKS WITH HERBED GARLIC BUTTER

Herbed Garlic Butter
¼ cup soft butter
1 Tbsp. minced shallot,
  green onion or chives
1 clove garlic, minced
2 Tbsp. minced parsley
Freshly ground pepper

Salmon Steaks
4 1-inch salmon steaks
¼ cup melted butter
Salt & pepper
2 lemons to garnish

Combine Herbed Garlic Butter ingredients, beating with a fork until well blended and fluffy.

Preheat broiler to 400 degrees F for 15 minutes. Dry salmon steaks with paper towel, then brush both sides with butter. Place on broiler pan and broil for 3 minutes on each side. Brush again with butter, sprinkle with salt and pepper and broil for 3 minutes. Turn, brush with butter and broil for 3 minutes or until salmon is firm and evenly pink in colour.

Transfer to a warmed serving platter, spread with herbed garlic butter and garnish with lemon wedges.

Serves 4.

— *Sheila Wilson*
Huntsville, Ontario

BROILED OYSTERS UNDER BUTTERED CRUMBS

18 oysters, drained with juice
  reserved
Lemon juice
2 Tbsp. chopped green pepper
2 Tbsp. chopped celery
1 green onion, chopped
2 Tbsp. bacon drippings

½ tsp. salt
1 cup oyster juice (water added
  if necessary)
½ cup chili sauce
¼ tsp. thyme
2 Tbsp. anisette
1 cup toasted buttered bread crumbs

Dry oysters and place in shallow greased baking dish one layer deep. Sprinkle with lemon juice and broil 3 to 4 inches from heat for 5 minutes or until oysters curl.

Meanwhile, sauté vegetables in bacon drippings until almost transparent. Add salt, oyster juice, chili sauce and thyme. Cook slowly until vegetables are tender, then pour over oysters. Sprinkle with anisette and cover evenly with buttered crumbs. Return to broiler for 15 minutes or until crust is brown and mixture is bubbly.

Serves 6.

— *Dianne Vanderberg*
Qualicum Beach, British Columbia

FISH KABOBS

⅓ cup soya sauce
2 Tbsp. brown sugar
1 tsp. ground ginger
1 clove garlic, crushed
1 tsp. dry mustard

¼ cup dry sherry
15-oz. can pineapple chunks with juice
2 lbs. halibut fillets, cut into 1½-inch
  cubes
2 dozen cherry tomatoes

Combine soya sauce, sugar, ginger, garlic, mustard, sherry and pineapple juice, and marinate fish in this for 2 hours. Meanwhile, soak 6- to 8-inch wooden skewers in water. Drain marinade from fish and alternate on skewers with chunks of pineapple and tomatoes. Bake in shallow pan at 350 degrees F for about 20 minutes or until fish flakes easily.

Serves 6 to 8.

— *Jane Lewis*
Grand River, Nova Scotia

GREEK-STYLE SKEWERED FISH

3 Tbsp. lime juice
1 Tbsp. olive oil
1 Tbsp. white wine
1 clove garlic, minced
½ tsp. basil

½ tsp. oregano
1 lb. fish fillets, cut into 1½-inch cubes
1 large red or green bell pepper
Lime wedges to garnish

Combine lemon juice, olive oil, wine, garlic, basil and oregano. Marinate fish in this for one hour. Cut pepper into chunks. Drain fish, reserving marinade. Thread fish and pepper chunks onto metal skewers or wooden ones that have been soaked in water for 1 hour. Place in a shallow pan and bake at 400 degrees F for 10 to 15 minutes, basting frequently with marinade. Serve with wedges of lime. This dish can also be barbecued.

Serves 4.

— Nan Millette
Corunna, Ontario

MARINATED BARBECUED FISH

⅓ cup soya sauce
2 Tbsp. vinegar
2 Tbsp. lemon juice
2 cloves garlic, crushed

1 lb. fresh fish fillets (perch, haddock, halibut)
¼ cup oil

Combine soya sauce, vinegar, lemon juice and garlic in a shallow glass dish. Place fillets, skin side down, in dish. Marinate for 2 hours. Arrange on a well-greased barbecue grill, brush with oil and cook until fish flakes easily. Fillets can also be baked at 400 degrees F for 20 minutes.

Serves 4.

— Louise Ogloend
Hjelmeland, Norway

SEAFOOD BEER BATTER

¾ cup flour
¼ cup cornstarch
1 tsp. baking powder
1 tsp. salt

¼ tsp. nutmeg
2 eggs
½ cup beer

Combine dry ingredients and mix. Lightly beat eggs and add along with beer. Beat until creamy smooth.

Use immediately to coat shrimp, oysters or other seafood for deep frying.

— Grace Hols
Houston, British Columbia

DEEP FRY BATTER

¾ cup cornstarch
½ cup flour
Salt & pepper

Water
1 tsp. baking powder

Mix flour and cornstarch with salt and pepper. Add enough water to make a thick batter. When ready to dip fish, add baking powder. Mix quickly, dip fish pieces and deep fry.

Makes enough for 1½ lbs. of fish fillets, which will serve 4 to 6 people.

— Irene Louden
Port Coquitlam, British Columbia

COD CHEEKS & TONGUES

2 lbs. cod cheeks & tongues
2 eggs
⅓ cup milk
Salt & pepper
⅓ cup flour

2 cups dry bread crumbs
2 Tbsp. butter
2 Tbsp. oil
Lemon wedges

Soak cheeks and tongues in salted cold water for ½ to 1 hour. Remove any tough adhering membranes.

Beat eggs and milk together in shallow bowl and season with salt and pepper.

Drain cheeks and tongues and pat dry. Roll in flour, dip in egg mixture, then coat with bread crumbs.

Heat butter and oil in large skillet. When very hot, add fish, and fry for 2 to 3 minutes on each side or until golden. Serve with lemon wedges.

Serves 4.

— *Judy Koster*
Bridgewater, Nova Scotia

BARBECUED STUFFED SALMON

2-4-lb. salmon
2-4 cups soft bread crumbs
½ cup chopped scallions
½ cup chopped celery
6-oz. can crab
½ lb. shrimp, cooked & shelled

1½ cups grated cheese
1 egg
½ cup chicken stock
1 tsp. oregano
1 tsp. basil

Rinse salmon and remove head, if desired. Open fish to expose cavity. With a sharp knife, slice next to the backbone through the small bones and flesh to within ¼ inch of skin. Do this the length of the fish.

Mix together remaining ingredients and stuff fish. Close opening with skewers or by sewing it shut.

Use a piece of 1-inch mesh chicken wire to enclose the salmon. Place salmon in wire over hot coals. Using aluminum foil, make a tent to place over fish to retain heat. Cook for 45 minutes to 1 hour, turning every 15 minutes.

Serves 4 to 6.

— *Cindy Shaver*
Cobble Hill, British Columbia

BARBECUED BUTTERFLY SALMON

4-lb. salmon, head removed
½ cup soya sauce
½ cup brown sugar

Butterfly salmon by cutting lengthwise along underside. Do not cut right through. Open fish, flesh side up.

Combine soya sauce and sugar, and spread generously over flesh.

Barbecue for 30 minutes — 20 minutes with skin side down and 10 with flesh side down.

Serves 6 to 8.

— *Barbara Wilkinson*
Winlaw, British Columbia

BARBECUED TROUT

½ onion, chopped
½ stalk celery, finely chopped
8 mushrooms, chopped
1 Tbsp. chopped chives
4 Tbsp. butter

1 tsp. parsley
Oregano
2 Tbsp. lemon juice
4 trout, cleaned

Sauté onion, celery, mushrooms and chives in 1 Tbsp. butter. Mix in parsley, oregano and ½ Tbsp. lemon juice.

Rinse and dry trout. Fill cavity with dressing, then close with skewer. Baste with remaining melted butter and lemon juice. Wrap in foil, and barbecue, basting frequently and turning once, for about 15 minutes over medium-low coals.

Serves 4.

— *Patricia Forrest*
Rosemont, Ontario

SHRIMP EN BROCHETTE

THIS RECIPE IS ALSO DELICIOUS MADE WITH SCALLOPS. IT CAN BE COOKED ON THE BARBECUE, IN which case skewers, not toothpicks, should be used to hold the shrimp and bacon together. Cook for 5 to 10 minutes.

10-12 slices bacon
Salt & pepper
8 oz. Roquefort cheese at room
   temperature

20-24 shrimp, shelled & deveined
Lemon slices
Parsley

Cut bacon slices in half crosswise, and sprinkle lightly with salt and pepper.

Beat cheese until creamy, then spread evenly on bacon slices. Roll 1 shrimp in each bacon slice and secure with a toothpick.

Broil shrimp 5 inches from heat for about 12 minutes, turning at least once.

Serve with lemon slices and parsley.

Makes 20 to 24 appetizers.

— *Pam Collacott*
North Gower, Ontario

TEMPURA BATTER

1½ cups flat beer
1 Tbsp. oil
2 eggs, separated

1 cup flour
1 tsp. salt

Combine 1 cup beer, oil and beaten egg yolks and beat well. Add flour and salt and mix until smooth. Refrigerate for at least 3 hours.

When ready to use batter, fold in stiffly beaten egg whites. Dip fish pieces in batter and deep-fry until golden brown on both sides.

Makes enough to coat 2 lbs. fish or seafood.

— *Maryanne Ashleigh*
St. Anne du Lac, Quebec

Sauces

They say a fish should swim thrice – first it should swim in the sea, then it should swim in butter and at last, sirrah, it should swim in good claret.

**– Polite Conversation
Jonathan Swift**

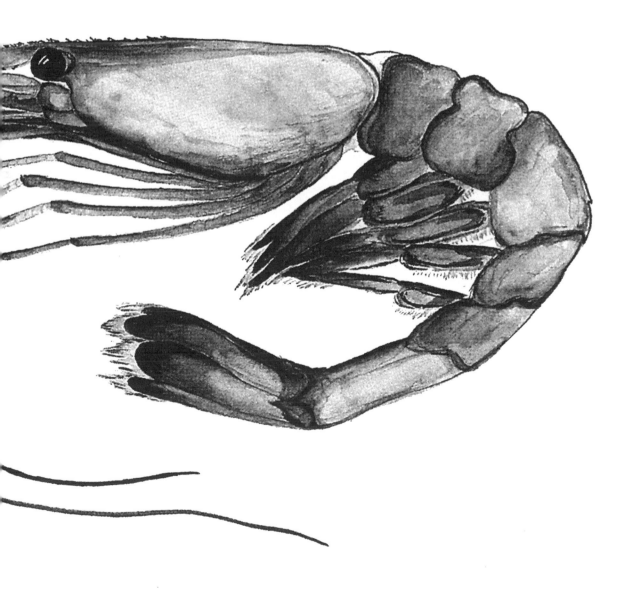

SEAFOOD COCKTAIL SAUCE

¾ cup tomato sauce
¼ cup grated horseradish
1 Tbsp. Worcestershire sauce
2 Tbsp. lemon juice

4-8 drops Tabasco sauce
Salt & pepper
1 tsp. sage
1 tsp. thyme

Combine all ingredients and mix well. Chill and serve with any kind of seafood.

Makes approximately 1 cup.

— Chris Nofziger
Elmworth, Alberta

CUCUMBER DILL SAUCE

THIS SAUCE IS ESPECIALLY DELICIOUS SERVED WITH COLD SALMON.

1 large cucumber
¾ tsp. salt
⅓ cup sour cream
⅓ cup mayonnaise
1 tsp. chopped dill weed

Peel cucumber, cut in half lengthwise and scrape out seeds. Shred finely, sprinkle with salt and chill for 2 hours.

Drain well and combine with sour cream, mayonnaise and dill.

Makes ⅔ cup.

— Sue Popoff
Castlegar, British Columbia

LEMON CUCUMBER SAUCE

THIS SAUCE, ALTHOUGH GOOD WITH ANY BAKED FISH, IS PARTICULARLY DELICIOUS SERVED with fish salad and fish mousse.

1 cup mayonnaise
1 cup grated, drained cucumber
3 Tbsp. lemon juice
½ tsp. dry mustard

½ tsp. salt
Pepper
2 Tbsp. chopped chives

Combine all ingredients and stir well.

Makes 1½ cups.

— Irene Louden
Port Coquitlam, British Columbia

CAPER SAUCE

¼ cup butter
1 Tbsp. lemon juice

1 Tbsp. capers
1 Tbsp. chopped parsley

Melt butter. Stir in remaining ingredients and mix well. Chill.

Makes ⅓ cup.

— Iris Bates
Midhurst, Ontario

TARTAR SAUCE

1 cup mayonnaise
2 Tbsp. minced capers
2 Tbsp. minced stuffed olives

1 Tbsp. chopped sweet pickle
1 Tbsp. chopped parsley

Combine all ingredients, mix well and chill. Serve with baked, broiled, pan-fried or deep-fried fish.

Makes 1¼ cups.

— Nan Millette
Corunna, Ontario

LUAU CURRY SAUCE

2 cups water
2 cups grated desiccated
  or fresh coconut
¼ cup vegetable oil
1 onion, chopped
2 apples, cored, peeled & diced

5 Tbsp. flour
1 tsp. salt
1 tsp. ginger
2 tsp. curry powder
3 Tbsp. soya sauce

Boil water, then pour over coconut and let stand for 20 minutes. Strain, discarding coconut. Meanwhile, heat oil, then add onion and apples. Cover and cook for 10 minutes.

Stir in flour, then add strained cocount milk and remaining ingredients. Reduce heat and cook for about 20 minutes or until thick and smooth.

Mix with 2 cups cooked seafood and serve over rice.

Serves 4.

— Helen Shepherd
Lansdowne, Ontario

SHELLFISH BUTTER

Shells of 8 boiled lobsters or 3-4 lbs.
  shrimp
8 oz. butter
Water

Pound shells to a pulp with a mortar and pestle. Add butter and work mixture until smooth.

Sauté over low heat, but do not allow mixture to brown. Add water to cover and bring to boil. Strain and discard shells.

Allow to cool, then remove butter from top.

— Alexis Matheson-Smith
White Rock, British Columbia

HOLLANDAISE SAUCE

HERE ARE TWO VARIATIONS OF HOLLANDAISE SAUCE — FIRST THE TRADITIONAL HAND-BEATEN method and second a recipe for blender Hollandaise, which loses a little in flavour but is much easier, especially for those intimidated by sauce making. Do not try either recipe in humid weather unless you use clarified butter, or they will curdle.

Traditional Hollandaise
½ cup butter
1½ Tbsp. lemon juice
3 egg yolks
4 Tbsp. boiling water
¼ tsp. salt
Cayenne

Melt butter slowly and keep it warm. In another pan, heat lemon juice until just warm.

Place egg yolks in top of double boiler over hot water. Beat with wire whisk until they start to thicken. Add 1 Tbsp. boiling water, continuing to beat until the eggs begin to thicken. Following the same method, continue adding water, 1 Tbsp. at a time, until all 4 Tbsp. have been used. Beat in warm lemon juice. Remove from heat and continue beating the sauce while slowly adding butter, salt and cayenne. Beat until sauce is thick. Serve immediately.

Makes approximately 1 cup.

Blender Hollandaise
½ cup butter
3 egg yolks
2 Tbsp. lemon juice
Cayenne
¼ tsp. salt

Heat butter until bubbly, but do not let it brown. Blend remaining ingredients in blender on high for 3 seconds, remove lid and pour in butter in a steady stream, continuing to blend on high. Sauce should be thickened and ready within 30 seconds. If it is not to be used at once, immerse blender in warm water.

Makes approximately 1 cup.

BASIC MAYONNAISE

THERE ARE MANY POSSIBLE ADDITIONS TO THIS BASIC MAYONNAISE. THE ONLY LIMITATION IS THE imagination of the cook. A few possibilities are garlic, curry powder, tarragon, different flavoured vinegars to make up part of the lemon juice, and different oils. Flavourings should be placed in the blender for the initial blending.

2 eggs
2 tsp. dry mustard
1 tsp. salt

2½ cups olive oil
6 Tbsp. lemon juice

Place eggs, mustard, salt and ½ cup oil in blender. Cover and blend on high until combined. Remove lid, and with blender still running, slowly add 1 cup oil, then lemon juice. When well blended, add remaining oil until mayonnaise is thick.

Makes approximately 3½ cups.

MAYONNAISE TARRAGON SAUCE

1½ cups mayonnaise
¾ cup sour cream or yogurt
3 Tbsp. finely chopped tarragon
2½ Tbsp. lemon juice

1½ Tbsp. tarragon vinegar
1½ Tbsp. grated onion
Salt

Combine all ingredients and mix well. Chill for at least 20 minutes.

Makes approximately 2½ cups.

ESCOFFIER SAUCE

½ cup walnuts
4 Tbsp. finely grated horseradish
1 tsp. sugar

Salt
Juice of 1 lemon
1 cup whipping cream

Pour boiling water over walnuts, then pick off skins when cool enough to handle. (This is slow and fiddly, but important.) Place skinned nuts in blender or food processor and chop briefly.

Add horseradish, sugar, salt, lemon juice and whipping cream. Blend briefly.

Makes approximately 2 cups.

— Lynne Roe
Orangeville, Ontario

SAUCE VERTE

10 leaves spinach
10 sprigs watercress
4 sprigs tarragon
4 sprigs parsley

2 sprigs dill feathers
2 egg yolks
8-10 oz. oil
Wine vinegar

Wash spinach, watercress, tarragon, parsley and dill. Chop coarsely. Steep in boiling water for 2 to 3 minutes, strain, then dry. Beat together egg yolks and oil until thick. Add a few drops of vinegar and blend until mixture has texture of mayonnaise. Add herbs and mix well.

Makes approximately 2 cups.

— Lynne Roe
Orangeville, Ontario

Index